DISASTERS SERIE

CONNECTICUT
DISASTERS

TRUE STORIES OF
TRAGEDY AND SURVIVAL

Ellsworth S. Grant

INSIDERS' GUIDE®

GUILFORD, CONNECTICUT
AN IMPRINT OF THE GLOBE PEQUOT PRESS

INSIDERS' GUIDE®

Text design by Pettistudio LLC, www.pettistudio.com
Map by M. A. Dubé © Morris Book Publishing, LLC

Library of Congress Cataloging-in-Publication Data
Grant, Ellsworth S.
  Connecticut disasters : true stories of tragedy and survival /
Ellsworth Grant. — 1st ed.
    p. cm.
  Includes bibliographical references.
  ISBN-13: 978-0-7627-3972-1 (alk. paper)
  ISBN-10: 0-7627-3972-X (alk. paper)
    1. Natural disasters—Connecticut—History. 2. Disasters—Connecticut—History. I. Title.
  GB5010.G73 2006
  363.3409746—dc22

                                                          2006014929

Manufactured in the United States of America
First Edition/First Printing

Contents

Acknowledgments

Of great assistance have been the following: Nancy Finlay, Curator of Graphics at Connecticut Historical Society; Judith E. Johnson, head researcher at the Connecticut Historical Society Library, and her capable assistant Jill Adams; Dr. Ralph Arcari of the University of Connecticut Health Center; Carl F. Bard, Deputy Commissioner, Department of Transportation; Christopher Collier, former State Historian; Betty Dempsey of Clemow Associates; Donald Engley, former librarian at Trinity College; Joel Lang of *Northeast* Magazine; Brenda Milkofsky, curator of Connecticut River Museum in Essex; and finally Mike Urban, Amy Paradysz, Dan Spinella, and The Globe Pequot Press for the opportunity to undertake this fascinating assignment.

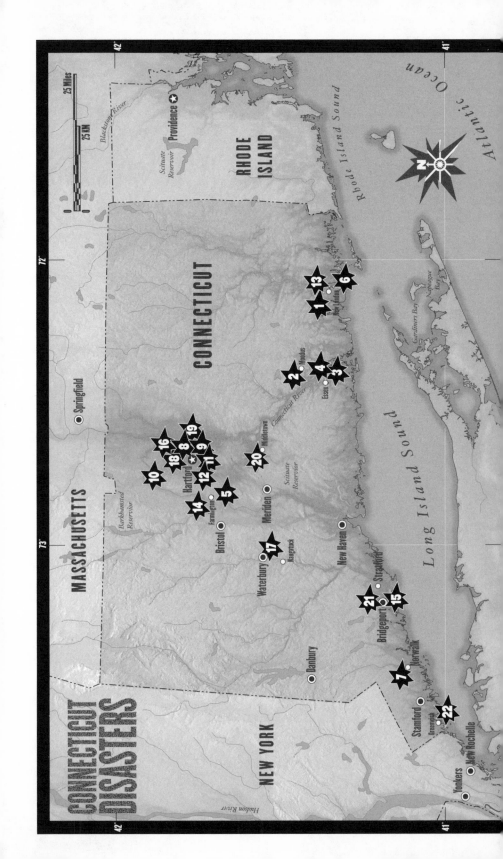

Preface

The original definition of *disaster* meant "ill-starred," the evil influence of a celestial body. Perhaps, once upon a time, but we know that disasters are either caused by humans or by nature. In the case of those selected for this book, eighteen were man-made and only seven were acts of nature.

Those made by human beings have been the most destructive of people and property, the result of poor judgment, faulty construction and engineering, negligence, inadequate inspection or oversight, economic change, and exploitation. Sometimes they serve to prevent similar occurrences; in other words, we learn from them through better design of boilers, bridges, roofs, and highways.

Natural disasters are not preventable, though their cumulative impact can be mitigated by flood control, early warnings, evacuations, and other means. The suddenness and significance of national disasters become imbedded in our memories. I will never forget where I was and what I was doing the day in 1941 when Pearl Harbor was attacked; the day in 1945 when Franklin Roosevelt died; the day in 1963 when John F. Kennedy was assassinated; or the day in 2001 when terror struck. Hurricane Katrina in September 2005 ranks as the number-one national catastrophe. When disaster strikes at that scale, people all over the nation are affected, as was Hartford after the 1906 earthquake in San Francisco. The Hartford alone paid $11.6 million to settle nearly 5,000 claims, equivalent to $200 million today.

But, thankfully, Connecticut has been spared calamities resulting in major loss of life, except for the flu pandemic of 1917–1918.

In every kind of disaster I have researched, what is most impressive and heart rending is the human response: terror, panic, disbelief, adaptability, looting, self-sacrifice, and heroism.

Undoubtedly, the first great disaster in New England at the start of the colonial era was the chicken pox epidemic in 1616 that ravaged the villages of Native Americans between Cape Cod and Penobscot Bay. This was soon followed by the small-pox epidemic from 1633 to 1665. In Europe and elsewhere communicable diseases for centuries had decimated popula-tions, and when the Europeans began to explore and settle North America, they brought with them such viruses as chicken pox, malaria, yellow fever, tuberculosis, and smallpox, to which, over many generations, their bodies had developed immunity. Not so the Indians. As a result, these diseases struck with rapid and horrible ferocity. Entire villages were wiped out, especially among the corn-growing Indians in southern New England. So many died, no one remained to bury the corpses.

The 1633 smallpox epidemic was even more lethal. About smallpox ravages among Native Americans, William Bradford, governor of the Plymouth Colony, wrote:

> They fall into a lamentable condition as they lie on their hard
> mats, the pox breaking and mattering and running into one
> another, their skin cleaving . . . to the mats . . . When they
> turn them, a whole side will flay off . . . and they will be all
> of a gore blood, most fearful to behold. . . . They die like rot-
> ten sheep.

By 1675 the Indian population had fallen from well over 70,000 to fewer then 12,000. The depopulation made it easier for the English to justify taking Indian cornfields. Gov. John Winthrop saw this as making room for settlement. "God," he said, "hath hereby cleared our title to this place."

In a few instances it has been impossible to find as much material as one would like to illuminate the account of the disaster, such as the Moodus earthquake. Newspapers in the eighteenth and early nineteenth centuries were not reportorial and often gave only the bare facts or did not report at all.

For a different reason this was also true of the influenza epidemic that occurred six months after the United States entered World War I. At the time the front pages had room only for what was happening in France. As a footnote to that account, I was a lucky survivor, having been born on October 8, 1917, in Wethersfield, which had no cases of flu, while nearby Hartford was one of the five cities hardest hit (550 deaths in that month).

I would have liked to write about the famine of 1816–1817. For sixteen months New England temperatures never rose above freezing, causing great distress for farmers, their crops, and their animals and spawning a new wave of emigration from Connecticut to other states such as Indiana and Ohio, in the hope the climate would be more salubrious. Between 1817 and 1820 their populations jumped nearly 50 percent. Samuel Goodrich, who lived through the ordeal, wrote that "thousands feared or felt that New England was destined to become a part of the frigid zone. . . . A sort of stampede took place from cold, desolate, worn out New England." They were mostly poor farming families with young children. What stories they could have told! Again, the newspapers seldom mentioned the hardships. The meteorological explanation for the disaster was the 1815 eruption of Tambora in the Malay archipelago, which threw 100 cubic miles of volcanic ash into the air.

When available, newspaper articles have helped to flesh out the accounts. As I read over the old files of the *Hartford Courant* and the defunct *Hartford Times*, I often marveled at the high quality of journalism in the eyewitness accounts of long-forgotten reporters.

TRAITOROUS FIRE

The Burning of New London

1781

During the American Revolution only one major battle was fought in Connecticut, although British redcoats had made several forays. In 1775 the warship HMS *Rose* bombarded Stonington in a futile quest for fresh meat. The royal governor of New York, William Tryon, twice led raids on Danbury to destroy patriot stores and saltworks and once on New Haven. But in September 1781, just before the defeat of Cornwallis at Yorktown, a British fleet sailed into New London Harbor, captured Forts Griswold and Trumbull, and burned the city to the ground.

What made the raid especially shocking to the citizens of New London was the identity of its leader, none other than the notorious Benedict Arnold, the same man who was once Gen. George Washington's ablest field commander, then the new nation's first traitor in September 1780, and by 1781 a brigadier general in the British navy. More galling was the fact that Arnold had been born in Norwich and moved to New Haven to become a druggist and wholesaler and leader of the state's first militia, which marched to Boston in 1775.

Fresh from raiding the coast of Virginia, Arnold was ordered by Sir Henry Clinton in New York to conduct a similar expedition against his native state. New London Harbor was full of privateers that had lately been the scourge of British merchant ships in Long Island Sound. Its most recent price, taken on July 31, was the *Hannah*, a richly laden vessel whose capture by Capt. Dudley Saltonstall particularly exasperated the British. Oddly enough, the leading merchant and shipbuilder, Nathaniel Shaw, had been a friend of Arnold's in prewar time.

Arnold's strategy was to enter the harbor secretly at night and destroy the shipping, the fortifications, and the public warehouses. Actually, the town received a warning about the expedition, but there had been so many false reports before, the inhabitants ignored the latest rumor and made no effort to defend themselves. The fleet of thirty-two ships arrived off the coast at 1 A.M. on September 6; twenty-four of them were transports carrying 1,852 men. Most of the force consisted of three regular regiments. A shift in the wind to the north prevented them from anchoring for eight hours, a delay that spoiled Arnold's hope for surprise.

In his report to the Admiralty later, Arnold said:

> Troops in two divisions and in four debarkations were landed around ten o'clock, one on each side of the harbor about three miles from New London. . . . The division on the New London side consisted of the 38th regiment, loyalist Americans, [General] Arnold's own American Legion, refugees [from Nova Scotia], and a detachment of 60 lagers [Hessian light infantry].

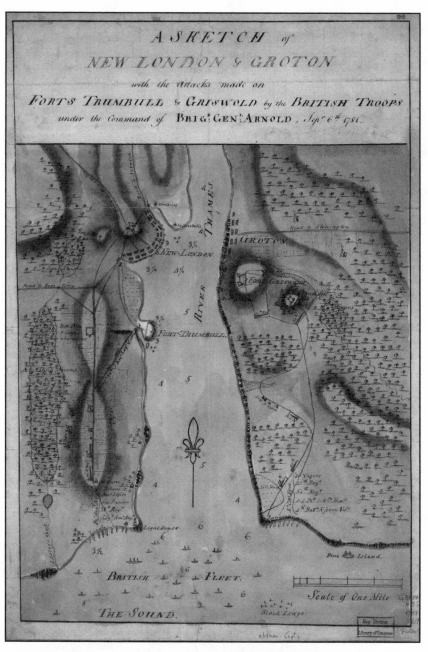

A sketch of New London and Groton with the attacks made on Forts Trumbull and Griswold by the British troops under the command of Benedict Arnold, September 6, 1781. LIBRARY OF CONGRESS, GEOGRAPHY AND MAP DIVISION

At dawn the fleet, still becalmed, was discovered lying off the entrance, and the transports trying to beat into the mouth of the Thames River. Col. William Ledyard was in command of the two forts, the harbor, and the towns of Groton and New London. An alarm was sounded from Fort Griswold. The startled citizens leapt from their beds and hastened to send away their families and most valuable possessions north: women and children in fields and woods carrying bags and pillowcases or driving cows, boys slinging stockings full of money over their shoulders, and carts laden with furniture and pets. At General Miller's, near the Norwich road, the dairy and larder were opened to feed everybody passing by.

In the harbor the privateer captains tried to secure their vessels by sailing upstream. At first they were frustrated by a contrary breeze and tide. Toward noon, however, before the enemy had taken the town, a favorable wind enabled a number to escape. Little could be done to move the contents of the warehouses to safety; Shaw's warehouse on Water Street was packed with goods from the rich cargo of the *Hannah,* and there was time only to fill one sloop.

Organizing a defense force was chaotic. About one hundred men were hastily armed. Lacking a commander and no plan of action, this force fled before Arnold's oncoming troops, who had disembarked west of the harbor light and marched toward Fort Trumbull. It was now 11 A.M. Designed only to repel a naval force, the fort could offer little resistance to five companies of redcoats. Its twenty-three soldiers fired one volley, spiked the guns, and then embarked in small boats to cross the river to Fort Griswold. A British man-of-war was so near that its crew fired muskets at the fleeing Americans and wounded seven.

Ashore, Arnold's green-coated Hessians secured the beach and led the way up Ocean Avenue, 3 miles from the town. Pressing forward on horseback with his main body of troops, Arnold reached a height of ground from which, using his spyglass, he could observe the houses and shops and the sails of American merchant ships heading toward Norwich, a familiar scene to one who had grown up in that environment. Said Arnold in his report: "No time was lost in gaining the town of New London. We were opposed by a small body of the enemy with one field piece, who were so hard pressed that they were obliged to leave."

On Blackball Street lived a well-to-do man named Manuring. Soldiers ransacked his house and tried to burn it, but after they left, a neighbor extinguished the flames with a barrel of soap. When the owner returned that night, he found a very young British soldier lying on a bed, calling for water, dying. Lieutenant Colonel Uphill, commanding the New Jersey loyalists, wrote: "We proceed to the town, constantly skirmishing with rebels who fled from hill to hill and stone fences." His men set fire to Picket Latimer's house, full of goods left there for safekeeping, the first house to be so consumed.

At the north end of town the destruction continued—beginning with the printing office and town mill. A detachment of soldiers went on to Winthrop's Neck, setting ablaze the Plumb house and every building around it. Only one home was spared, Capt. Guy Richard's, where his daughter lay ill. Listening to the pleas of those attending her, the officer left her and the house alone. Coming up to Colonel Uphill's men, Arnold extended his sword toward Water Street and its concentration of shops and warehouse, shouting, "Soldiers! Do your duty."

And they did. Shops, stores, dwellings, piles of lumber, wharves, and ten or twelve vessels were soon enveloped in flames. Irish butter melted, trickled along the street, and filled the gutters. A privateer sloop, fitted for a cruise, was burnt until she drifted away and sank. At the same time, in the coves at the south end of the town, all the fishing craft were set afire.

A humane officer spared the houses on Bradley Street when told the street was the Widow's Row. But not the market wharf, the old magazine and battery, the courthouse, the jail, and the Episcopal church. Before fleeing, the landlady of a tavern whose husband was a sergeant in the militia and her brother a British officer prepared a sumptuous dinner for the latter.

Arnold himself stopped by to eat a hasty meal with an old acquaintance on Bank Street, a Loyalist named James Tilley. Not far away, at Shaw's Wharf, the *Hannah* was set afire, the powder aboard exploding and sending flames up Bank Street. Before they rose from the table, Tilley's house was ablaze. Nearby, as Arnold knew, was the stone residence and wooden office of his former compatriot Nathaniel Shaw. His men set fire to the office. The flames spread to the roof but were extinguished by a neighbor who found a barrel of vinegar in the garret and poured it on the blaze. But the whole of Bank Street, the town's wealthiest section, paid dearly, mainly because, as Arnold reported, several of the stores were filled with gunpowder. "The explosion of the powder and the change of wind soon after the stores were fired communicated the flames to part of the town, which was, notwithstanding every effort to prevent it, unfortunately destroyed."

To his credit Arnold had forbidden his troops to plunder private property or molest the inhabitants. To the discredit of

New London, there was considerable plundering of the warehouses and homes by "a few worthless vagrants," as the historian Frances Caulking called them.

The British finished raiding by 4 P.M. Arnold's fleet sailed out of New London the next morning. According to Dr. Walter L. Power, author of *Murder or Mayhem?*, the damage totaled 143 buildings, including 65 houses. Their owners were later compensated with land grants in the state's Western Reserve (Ohio). Nearly one hundred families were left homeless. Fortunately, only four American lost their lives and fewer than a dozen were wounded. Despite his inclination toward humaneness and forbearance, the people of New London never forgave nor forgot the traitor branded forever as Benedict Arnold, the "Dark Eagle."

The battle of Fort Griswold in Groton the same afternoon was Connecticut's worst defeat in the war. Col. William Ledyard was brutally killed after surrendering. Six other Americans were killed and 20 wounded, but the redcoats had almost 200 casualties, 48 of them fatal.

SHAKES AND MOANS

The Moodus Earthquake

1791

Who ever heard of an earthquake in New England? California, yes, but certainly not Connecticut! Yet earthquakes of a moderate type have occurred in Connecticut for nearly 300 years. The earliest was recorded in Gov. John Winthrop's journal on June 1, 1638:

> Between three and four in the afternoon . . . there was a great earthquake. It came with a noise like continual thunder, or the rattling of coaches in London. . . . It shook the ships which rode in the harbor all the islands. The noise and shaking continued about four minutes.

Long ago, before the coming of white men, the Connecticut River Valley was occupied by a number of river-based tribes of American Indians. Adraien Block, who discovered the Connecticut River in 1614, called them the "Sequins." They were later called Wangunks and dominated the area stretching from

Essex all the way to Middletown, their headquarters. The Wangunk clan living in Haddam and East Haddam was much given to "worshipping the devil," their strange religious ceremonies undoubtedly inspired by the famous "Moodus noises."

The village of Moodus in the south-central part of the state takes its name from the Indian word *machimoodus* or "place of noises." Tremors and shocks were described as early as 1702 by the Reverend Jeremiah Hobart as "strange bellowing" and in 1729 by the Reverend Stephen Hosmer as "the noise of a cannon shot or severe thunder." Hosmer said in a letter to a friend:

> As to earthquakes, I have something considerable and awful to tell you. Earthquakes have been here, as has been observed for more than 30 years. . . . Before the English settlement there were great numbers of Indian inhabitants, and that it was a place of extraordinary pawaws, or in short . . . where the Indians drove a prodigious trade in worshipping the devil. . . . Many years past an old Indian was asked the reason of the noises in this place to which he replied that "the Indians' God was very angry that the Englishman's God was come there."
>
> Now, whether there be anything diabolical in these things, I know not. . . . Whether it be fire or air distressed in the caverns of the earth cannot be known; for there is no eruption, no explosion perceptible but by sounds and tremors, which sometimes are very fearful and dreadful. . . . I have, I suppose heard several hundred of them within twenty years. . . . Sometimes we have heard them almost every day, and great numbers of them within the space of a year.

On the evening of May 16, 1791, the ground began shaking violently. An eyewitness recalled it this way: "It began at 8 o'clock with two very heavy shocks in quick succession. The first was the most powerful; the earth appeared to undergo very violent convulsions."

Stone walls collapsed, chimneys fell, latched doors flew open. The captain of a ship at anchor in Killingworth saw fish jump out of the water. The next morning, there was a great fissure in the ground several rods long. The first shock was felt as far away as Boston and New York, the second at a distance of 70 miles. Consternation and dread filled every house. During the night there followed a succession of twenty or thirty smaller shocks. The next day, stones of several tons were found displaced; apertures and fissures showed where the explosions originated.

The eruption came from Mount Tom, a "bold hill" about 2^1/$_2$ miles north of East Haddam and in the triangular neck of land between the Salmon and Moodus Rivers. This mountain was sacred to the Wangunks, who called it Machimoodus, the place where the evil spirit Hobomoko lived in a cavern. For generations the Indians had been used to lesser shocks. According to legend the "noises" began when Hobomoko failed to end his power struggle with the black magic witches of Devil's Hopyard, 5 miles east. The fights took place under Mount Tom in a cavern lighted by a great carbuncle, a glowing net.

News of the 1791 earthquake spread widely, and visitors frequently came to the area in the hope of hearing more noises. No one could solve the puzzle of its origin. Then one day there appeared a queer old gentleman whose questions and actions, the residents hoped, would shed light on the mystery. Claiming to be Dr. Steel of Great Britain, he insisted there was a large jewel, the witches' carbuncle, buried in Mount Tom, and in some mystical way this was causing the noises. To prove his theory he ensconced himself in an empty blacksmith shop nearby, locking the doors and covering all the windows. At night people heard clanging hammers, and show-ers of sparks shot from the chimney. For weeks the wizard labored. At last, one evening watchers saw the doctor steal silently out toward Mount Tom. Reaching the topmost rock, he began with pick and shovel to pry at the rock, whispering incantations. Suddenly, the rock moved and from the deep hole underneath, the carbuncle blazed in the midnight sky, and the noises roared as never before. The watchers fled for their lives.

The next morning Dr. Steel and his mysterious treasure had disappeared. According to the legend he escaped down the Connecticut River and was soon aboard a ship bound for Eng-land. He may have quieted Mount Tom for a while and brought peace and quiet to Moodus, but he profited not from the jewel, it was said. His ship foundered, and all aboard were lost.

Since 1791 there have been frequent tiny earthquakes. The mid-nineteenth-century historian John de Forest wrote that "strange noises and rumblings have been heard at times in the bowels of Mount Tom . . . and slight shocks, as of an earth-quake, have been felt through the surrounding country. . . . The astonished inhabitants have heard sounds like slow thun-der rolling down from the north and at last closing with a loud report which shook the houses and everything in them."

There were similar disturbances in 1917 and 1968, shaking houses and rattling windows. During the 1980s tremors too small to be noticed were recorded on instruments more than 500 times. Although, as far as is known, the Moodus noises never caused fatalities, they did result in a lot of property damage and a great deal of fear, panic, and wonderment among the inhabitants.

Geologists rank Moodus as one of the most active earthquake zones in New England. The seismic activity is caused by the shifting of the earth's crust along a fault, causing sections of bedrock to slide past each other, bumping and grinding and making eerie noises. The Moodus fault appears to be part of a larger fault that stretches from New Haven eastward, although it has not been positively identified. It is there but can't be seen. Yet the "noises" will surely continue and may one day, with Hobomoko's spiritual help, culminate in another full-blown earthquake.

THE BRITISH ARE COMING!

The Raid on Essex
1814

For two hundred years, shipbuilding, next to farming, was the most important economic activity on the Connecticut River. In the small towns from Lyme to South Windsor, family-owned shipyards crafted wooden sailing vessels, mostly schooners and brigs. They accounted for an estimated 4,000 commercial and military ships. More tonnage slid down their ways than either in New London or New Haven. The period between the American Revolution and the War of 1812 was especially profitable. Essex alone boasted of having ten shipyards, the largest of which was operated by the Hayden family.

The good times came to an abrupt halt when President Thomas Jefferson tried to put an end to the British navy's dominance of the high seas. In 1807 Congress passed the Embargo Act, forbidding all American exports. The act had a devastating effect on the ports in Connecticut and along the East Coast. Moreover, it had no influence on changing English policy or on protecting the U.S. merchant marine from the seizure of its sailors. In June 1812 these conditions led to the second war with Britain. In New England it was bitterly referred to as "Mr. Madison's War" and almost caused secession.

So, thirty-three years after the burning of New London, the redcoats were back in Long Island Sound with their warships. In 1814 their main purpose was to destroy the pesky, fast-sailing privateers that harassed their supply ships. As during the American Revolution, the sometimes profitable task of "twisting the lion's tail" fell to Connecticut-built vessels. They were more effective than ever; royal frigates could not compete in speed and maneuverability with swift, slender sloops and schooners that sailed close to the wind. Many were built in Essex, as the British were well aware. So disruptive were they to the naval blockade on Long Island Sound that retaliation was inevitable.

What happened on April 8 and 9 is vividly described in the report of Capt. Richard Coote, commanding officer of the sloop HMS *Borer,* to his superior Capt. T. B. Capel of HMS *La Hogue,* anchored off New London, as quoted in the *Connecticut Gazette:*

> I have the honor to acquaint you that in obedience to your Order of the 7th instant directing me to take charge of a detachment of Boats for the purpose of taking or destroying a number of Vessels building and equipping sad Privateers and Letters of Marque in Connecticut River, I proceeded to His Majesty's sloop under my command on the evening of that day . . . and I have now the pleasure of informing you that thro' the steady and indefatigable exertions of the Officers and Men under my Orders, the Service has been accomplished in a more effectual way than my most sanguine hopes had led me to expect.

His sloop anchored off Saybrook at 9:45 P.M., towing three barges, two gigs, and a pinnace. The northerly wind held them

Wood engraving by John Warner Barber of a canal boat, ca. 1820s.
CONNECTICUT HISTORICAL SOCIETY MUSEUM

back, but the tide was flooding, and they began to row the 6 miles upriver to Essex, then called Potapaug, reaching the village about 3:30 A.M. Coote reported:

> On approaching, we found the town alarmed, the Militia all on alert and apparently disposed with the assistance of one 4 lb. Gun to oppose our landing, however after the discharge of the Boats' Guns and a volley of musketry from our Marines, they prudently ceased firing and gave us no further interruption.

Some 200 marines, commanded by Lieutenant Lloyd, landed and formed on Main Street. The sailors warped the vessels alongside the wharf into the river and those in stocks were burned. At daylight other vessels were seen at moorings upstream and set afire. Stores of marine supplies were either destroyed or removed to the American brig *Young Anaconda* and the schooner *Eagle*, both of which Coote deemed worthy of taking away.

By 10 A.M. the raiders were ready to embark, but a contrary wind and enemy fire from the opposite shore forced the British to burn both of their prizes. Coote decided to defer his retreat until dark:

> Large fires were alight on each side to show the situation of the Boats, and Vessels filled with armed men were anchored in the River, all these commenced a brisk but ill directed fire. . . . At one-half past eight we were abreast of the lowest Fort [Saybrook] . . . and here they made final and ineffectual effort to detain us. The Boats passed in triumph leaving our enemies to lament.

A few days later the *Connecticut Gazette* reported its version of the raid:

> It is with grief and mortification we perform the task of announcing to our readers that on Friday morning last, four of the enemy's barges and the launches . . . proceeded up the Connecticut River to Potapaug Point and destroyed upward of 20 sail of vessels, without sustaining the loss of a single man. . . .
>
> The inhabitants were in great consternation, but Capt. Coote informed them that . . . if his party were not fired upon no harm should fall . . . and a mutual understanding of that purport was agreed to. . . . The enemy immediately commenced the act of burning the vessels. . . . Their conduct towards the inhabitants was unexceptionable, except that some clothes and plate were taken by a person supposed to be an American who . . . acted as pilot and guide and had frequently been there with fish for sale.

Indeed, the eight-oared barges had been guided by a traitor, who was paid $2,000 for his services, equal to half a million dollars today.

It is true that the inhabitants were not molested. The British officer in charge said his orders were only to burn the vessels in the harbor, but if any of the soldiers were insulted or killed, they would burn every house in the village. But the people were frightened, and some fled from the waterfront with their most prized possessions. According to fifteen-year-old Austin Lay, a few marines fired indiscriminately at the houses. He went down to the *Osage* at the wharf and tried to put out the fire but was thwarted by a British officer who drew his sword and threatened to cut out his tongue. Several articles of plate were stolen, but the officers made their men return them. They did seize seven hogshead of rum and some cordage belonging to Samuel Hayden.

To separate legend from fact is difficult. One legend has it that the marines entered the tap room of Uriah Hayden's house, where a few frightened militia were hiding, and swiped the rum supply. The Hayden family operated the largest shipyard. Another, more intriguing, legend is that the town was saved by Captain Coote's encounter with an American officer on Main Street; extending his hand, the American gave the secret shake of the Masonic Order, and the British commander returned it. Coote, it is also said, was fearful about being able to find his way downriver, and when Jeremiah Glover, an Essex boatman, beseeched him to spare his sloop, Coote agreed on condition that Glover act as his pilot. Shaking with fear, Glover lay in the bottom of the barge while the Americans fired furiously from Saybrook Point. Unharmed, he was landed on Fisher's Island.

The official British report does not mention casualties, but at least two of the invading force were killed when leaving the river. About a year later a visitor to Plum Island, across the Sound, saw eleven recent graves, which the lighthouse keeper told him were those of men killed on the raid and buried by Captain Coote.

The number of ships burned totaled twenty, some claim as many as twenty-eight, only four of which, it turned out, were privateers. The rest were merchantmen. The *New Haven Register* listed twenty-one: five ships, five schooners, eight sloops, and three brigs. The losses of more than 5,000 tons of shipping, however, affected numerous families and ended Essex's shipbuilding for some time. It ruined, for instance, the career of Capt. Richard Hayden, Uriah's nephew. The maritime trade never recovered, but shipbuilding prospered until midcentury, thanks to the cotton trade and the introduction of transatlantic packets (passenger ships). Cotton emerged as the country's leading export. The primary market? Great Britain!

SMOKE ON THE WATER

Deadly Steamboats
1833 and 1840

A new era of marine power began when in 1815 the little steamboat *Fulton* arrived in New Haven. Rigged as a sloop in case sails were needed, as they often were in the first days of steam power, she made a dreadful din, the result of the thrash of her paddles and the sharp, staccato blasts of her wood-fired engine, as steam escaped from the cylinder. Sixty passengers made the trip from New York at a fee of $6.00 each. Subsequently, as the *Fulton* churned up the Connecticut River, villagers rushed to the banks to see the new-fangled contraption "coming on wheels in the water."

Soon steamboats were making regular runs between Hartford and New York. In 1824 the Connecticut Steamboat Company's side-wheeler *Oliver Ellsworth* went into service, the first of a long line of "floating palaces." She was 127 feet long and carried sixty-two passengers in separate cabins for ladies and gentlemen. That same year, the Marquis de Lafayette, on his farewell visit to New England, came aboard "amid the salute of cannon and the shouts of thousands of gratified and grateful spectators." But with their crude crosshead engines and undependable copper boilers, travel on steamboats was at best a hazardous undertaking. On a March night in 1827 in Long Island Sound the *Oliver Ellsworth's* boiler exploded, killing a fireman and injuring several passengers. She managed to sail to the Saybrook town dock; from there an excited post rider galloped to Hartford, burst into the sitting legislature, and exclaimed: "The *Eliver Ollsworth* biled her buster!" Repaired with a new copper boiler, the *Oliver Ellsworth* soon resumed her regular schedule.

Business became highly profitable and competitive. The Hartford Steamboat Company attracted passengers with the new *Macdonough*, larger than the *Ellsworth*, with seventy-six berths. The two companies decided to share the Hartford–New York route by running on different days. Both stopped at a number of river landings. The 150-mile trip to New York cost $5.00 and took about fifteen hours, a lot faster than the stagecoach. In 1833 the *Macdonough* was supplanted by the *New England*, at 261 tons and 153 feet long, "with two copper boilers of great strength." Her engine and boilers were made at West Point. No expense had been spared to make her as safe and strong as possible. That same fateful year, Commodore Cornelius Vanderbilt of New York, intent on establishing a steamboat monopoly, pitted his faster *Water Witch* against the *New England* and cut fares from $5.00 to $1.00.

On October 8, 1833, the worst steamboat disaster on the Connecticut River occurred. Thirteen perished. The previous afternoon the *New England* left New York for Hartford in the company of the steamboat *Boston*. In Long Island Sound she gradually pulled ahead of her companion. Some passengers felt uneasy about the competition to be first, but there did not seem to be any unusual press of steam pressure. The *New Eng-*

land reached the mouth of the Connecticut River about 1 A.M. At Saybrook some difficulty occurred with the engine, causing the crew to throw out the anchor to prevent drifting ashore.

Thirty minutes later, the problem seemed corrected, so she proceeded upriver about 8 miles, to Essex, arriving at 3 A.M. The night was excessively dark, and the rain poured in torrents. The *New England*'s engine was stopped, a small boat was lowered to land a passenger, and then it happened. Both boilers exploded with a noise like heavy cannon. The shock was dreadful. The steam blast extinguished the lights on deck and in the cabins. Dock hands on shore saw the desolation and horror aboard and heard the groans and shrieks of the wounded and dying.

There were about seventy passengers aboard, most of them in their berths, in addition to twenty crewmen. Those on deck or abed in the ladies' cabins were fortunate, but those on cots opposite the cabin doors and some who, at the first alarm, sprang from their beds were scalded. No one outside the ladies' cabins could have survived. All on deck abaft the boilers were either killed or wounded. Captain Waterman was in the wheelhouse watching the landing of the passenger from the small boat. Sensing a movement over the boilers, he jumped to the forward deck, suffering only bruises. Somehow he maneuvered his vessel to the wharf thirty minutes later.

The people of Essex were aroused and did what they could to care for the injured. Several physicians attended the five crewmen, including the chambermaid Jane Pruden, as well as six passengers scalded or otherwise injured. Miss Pruden, sleeping in the upper berth next to the larboard (port) boiler, was thrown out and fell upon her hands in the water.

As soon as the news reached Hartford, the owners dispatched the *Massachusetts* to pick up the survivors. Of the thirteen who died, five were crewmen. Two of the eight passengers killed were women. Forty feet from the boilers in the most remote berth slept a Mrs. Thompson with her three young children; the youngest died with her. The other two, though scalded, survived. The mother's clothes were so hot, they burned the hands of a would-be rescuer. Letters she had written were charred by the steam.

A gentleman passenger from Middletown wrote:

Our journey in the steamboat New England was very pleasant, last evening, until we entered the Connecticut River. At about one o'clock, this morning, when we were all asleep, myself excepted, I perceived the engine, or something else, was out of order. I was in the forward cabin and concluded I was in the safest part of the boat. Things seemed to go on badly until 3 o'clock. When both boilers burst simultaneously . . . the result was two persons were killed outright, about 25 wounded or scalded—out of which number five or six may not survive. The destruction of the upper works was almost entire.

The next day the same man added in a second letter:

A steamboat was sent down [from Hartford] to the scene of distress; she returned . . . with the news of four deaths, and that eight or ten more must die with their wounds, and perhaps more. The upper works . . . present the most extraordinary wreck I ever beheld, and if the event had occurred in the daytime when the passengers are generally upon the decks, not a person could have escaped injury.

This acute observer pointed to the possible cause of the disaster:

When she found it necessary to lay to fix her steering ropes, I at once became astonished that she did not throw off steam, as is usually the case when stops are made; and from this to the time of the explosion, there were several stops made [but] I could perceive but a faint sound of the discharge of steam.

After the explosion he found himself unhurt and got on his clothes. The docks were covered with broken timber, the river full of baggage, and the air full of the cries of misery and the moans of the dying. An eyewitness ashore, perhaps a marine expert, described the wreck:

She seems the slaughter house of the traveler. . . . You stand astonished at the force and effect of the murderous explosion. From the stem to the wheel-room, all is well; from the wheel-room aft, athwart the deck and downward to the water, you see the direction as well as the power of the blast. The guards on deck, extending beyond the hull upon which the boilers were placed, were blown through; beams of a foot square supported by braces and knees were blown off as square and close to the hull as if sawed by a carpenter.

The board appointed to examine the cause laid the blame on the substitute engineer. The veteran regular engineer, Mr. Potter, was not aboard on this trip, his place taken by a Mr. Marshall from the West Point Foundry. Although he had the reputation of being a skilled professional, his statement that

the boilers had only 8 or 10 inches of steam on at the time of
the explosion was considered improbable in view of the destruction: both boilers rent asunder and thrown into the river,
the guards broken off, the promenade deck lifted, and the
ladies cabin and all the upper works completely shattered.

Oddly enough, the engine was not affected, but the steam
pipe was broken at its junction with the main steam pipe in the
engine room. The safety valve, which tells the engineer the
amount of pressure, was still in good working order. Furthermore, the examiners were satisfied that the boilers had been
properly constructed. No flaws were found in the copper. In
short they concluded that the explosion resulted from the accu-
mulation of steam pressure to nearly 30 inches, a force on the
internal surface of each boiler of three million pounds.

Seven years later, on January 13, 1840, a worse steamboat disaster occurred, not on the Connecticut River but in Long Island
Sound. The *Lexington,* launched in April 1835, was Commodore Vanderbilt's pride and joy (of the two dozen steamboats he built). The fastest and largest steamer of the day, Ïshe
was 207 feet long, displaced 488 tons, and had a speed of from
12 to 14 knots. The *Hartford Courant* commented about her this
way: "Since her first trip has been almost as regular as the sun,
and as yet has never lost a trip, and very seldom been an hour
beyond her regular time, never met with the slightest accident,
blow high, blow low, fair or foul, sunshine or fog."

The next year, Vanderbilt, determined to beat his competi-
tors with newer boats and lower fares on the Hartford to New
York run, added the *Cleopatra* to his fleet, with 180 sleeping
berths and elaborate furnishings, His plan was to have *Lexington* and *Cleopatra* pioneer a regular daily line to New York. But

The Lexington *was bound for Stonington when she caught fire and sank on January 13, 1840. Most of the seventy-five aboard drowned or froze to death.*
COURTESY OF CONNECTICUT RIVER MUSEUM

for some unexplained reason, probably because he was losing money, in December 1938 he sold her to Robert Schuyler for $60,000. Schuyler headed the New Jersey Steam Navigation & Transportation Company, a competing line that served Stonington, Newport, and Providence.

On that frigid January 13 night, the *Lexington* was bound for Stonington, with a small number of passengers and 150 bales of cotton on her main deck. At 7:30 P.M. she caught fire and around 3 A.M. sank at Old Field Point, 61 miles east of New York, 16 miles beyond Eaton's Neck, and only 4 miles from shore. As might be expected in winter, she carried far fewer passengers than she would have in spring or summer; almost all of the seventy-five aboard were businessmen and crew members. Only one woman and child were identified. There were few survivors; most drowned or froze to death. Although the ship sank very early Tuesday morning, news of the tragedy did not reach New York until Wednesday. The next day, the company sent another steamboat to the scene and returned with five bodies, a load of trunks, bales of cotton, and other goods.

The New York coroner's inquest into the cause of the accident lasted nine days. The first witness was the former builder and owner, Commodore Vanderbilt, who testified that he had great confidence in *Lexington's* strength, but "it was so common a thing for a steamboat to take fire." Capt. William Comstock, general agent and superintendent of the New Jersey Company, agreed: "I considered her the boat best guarded against fire than anyone running out of New York. I cannot account for the fire." There was always danger of fire onboard, he added, because of the stoves for heating, the wood-burning kitchen range, and the oil lamps that lighted the salon and staterooms. He said, "Passengers are nowadays expected to have everything extravagant, and of course we were expected to furnish them with a lamp or light with which to retire."

He noted that the boat's fire engine, 60 feet of hose, and three dozen fire buckets on deck were all in perfect order. The engine was designed to pump water from the sea. Unlike earlier steamboats that burned wood, the *Lexington* burned coal, considered 50 percent safer and spark free. The boat had been inspected in October and given a certificate of soundness and seaworthiness. Inspector Ellis S. Bunker said that "had anyone onboard had presence of mind enough that with a bucket of water he might have put out the fire." Captain Comstock added that at the time of the inspection a few defects had been corrected, new flues were put into the boiler, and the smoke pipe insulated with sheets of iron.

When the alarm sounded at 7:30 that fateful night, the pilot, Captain Manchester, was at the wheel in the forward wheelhouse. Stepping outdoors, he saw dense smoke. Captain Child joined him and yelled, "Haul for the land." Together, they spun the wheel to starboard. By this time smoke and fire had risen from beneath the promenade or top deck into the wheelhouse, forcing them to abandon the wheel. *Lexington* carried three boats: a 24-foot lifeboat and two 20-foot "quarter" boats. The lifeboat was lowered, but the rope holding it to the bow parted and she was impaled under the wheel below. Then the two quarter boats were lowered and immediately lost. Now, with the flames 10 feet high, twenty-five or thirty officers, firemen, and waiters huddled on the forecastle. The deck was so hot from the fire underneath that some tried to cool it with water from a hand pump. Manchester shouted an order: "Open up the baggage crates, throw out the luggage and make a raft!" That effort failed: They couldn't tie the baggage crates together. Then, Manchester, deciding to abandon ship, climbed onto a bale of cotton with two others. Using a piece of plank from the bulwark, they paddled toward shore the rest of the night. At noon Manchester saw nearby the sloop *Merchant*, raised his handkerchief as a signal of distress, and passed out.

The second mate, David Crowley, managed to get ashore after spending forty-eight hours on a bale of cotton. Wednesday night he landed on the beach, crawled over the sand and ice, and walked almost a mile to the nearest home, his legs and feet badly frozen.

Another survivor was twenty-four-year-old Capt. Chester Hilliard, a native of Norwich, on his way home to visit his family. Twenty minutes after the alarm, he said the engine stopped. He urged the crew to throw the burning cotton overboard.

Finding only one bale unburned, he attached a line, slipped it overboard, and climbed on, together with a fireman named Cox. As Hilliard testified at the coroner's inquest:

> I gave him my vest as he had on only a flannel shirt. The wind was pretty fresh. Among the few still onboard was a lady whose child had fallen into the water. She cried out for us to save it. But the child was dead, a little girl with a bonnet. I was wet up to my middle. We were in sight of the boat until she went down at 3. It was so cold as to make it necessary for me to exert myself to keep warm by whipping my arms around my body. About four the bale capsized. Cox appeared to have given up all hope of being saved. I rubbed him and beat his flesh to keep his blood in circulation. The bale gave a lurch, and Cox slipped off, and I saw him no more.

He was finally rescued by the sloop *Merchant* and joined Captain Manchester, no worse for his ordeal.

The coroner's jury's verdict was that "the fire was communicated to the promenade deck by the intense heat of the smoke pipe or from sparks between the smoke pipe and steam chamber." It could have been extinguished, the jurors said, "if the hand buckets been manned at the start." The owners of *Lexington,* however, disputed the verdict. Claiming that the jurors were all ignorant of steamboat technology, they maintained that the fire originated neither between decks nor in the bales of cotton. Thus, what really happened was left embedded in mystery and obscurity.

In an amazing feat of nineteenth-century journalism, Currier & Ives produced a vivid print of the disaster three days later—its first bestseller. This success marked the beginning of the use of prints as a means of reporting current events.

CURSED LITTLE DITCH

The Ill-Fated Farmington Canal

1835

It was the largest single transportation project in Connecticut's history. It would extend from New Haven to Northampton, Massachusetts, and give New Haven a trade connection to northern New England that it badly needed to compete with its sister capital in Hartford. (Connecticut had two state capitals until 1876.) It brought in the first tidal wave of immigrants from Ireland to dig. Yet, tragically, it failed twenty years after completion.

After the second war with England and the end of the federalist party, the country experienced an "Era of Good Feeling." Leaders in Congress favored a protective tariff for manufacturers, a home market, and better transportation. "Let us," said John Calhoun in 1817, "bind the Republic together with a perfect system of roads and canals." That same year, New York began construction of the Erie Canal. When completed in 1825, it outstripped all eastern seaports as the best route to the Midwest.

In 1821, New Haven, realizing its port could no longer compete in trading with New England against the thriving towns along the Connecticut River, resolved to survey the country north through Farmington for a canal route. Under the skillful leadership of the lawyer James Hillhouse, representatives from seventeen towns met in Farmington the following January and resolved that the project "would afford great convenience, enhance the value of production of the country and enrich the population." A graduate of Yale in Nathan Hale's class of 1773, Hillhouse served in Congress during the administrations of Washington and Jefferson; New Haven would remember him best for planting the city's elms and laying out Grove Street Cemetery.

Benjamin Wright, chief engineer of the Erie Canal, was hired to undertake a rough survey and concluded that the proposed route was "favorably formed for a great work of this kind." The legislature granted a charter of incorporation to the Farmington Canal Company in May of 1822. Five commissioners, headed by Judge Simeon Baldwin, were appointed; the others were prominent New Haveners, including the inventor Eli Whitney. They estimated the cost of construction would be half a million dollars, 40 percent of which would be subscribed by the newly formed Mechanics Bank of New Haven. Soon, Massachusetts approved granting a charter in that state that would extend the route from Southwick to Northampton, allowing the canal to reach the Connecticut River. Another New Haven bank put up $100,000 for the Hampshire & Hampden Canal Company, and later the two companies merged. Their investors dreamed of a canal system that would someday even reach the St. Lawrence River in Canada!

Even though New Haven's elite supplied most of the capital as well as the administration for the canal, the original subscription for 1,000 shares did not meet the expectations of the

Canal Committee, a foreboding of trouble ahead. Finally, three years after incorporation, ground-breaking ceremonies took place on July 4, 1825, at Salmon Brook Village in Granby, attracting a crowd of more than 2,000. The New Haven delegates traveled in a boat, covered with a white awning and flag-decorated curtains, and drawn by four horses, which were frequently changed. Oliver Wolcott Jr., Connecticut's governor, spoke briefly, but another bad omen occurred when the spade he used to break ground broke.

Though Wolcott had shown himself a supporter of economic ventures, especially woolen mills, it is curious that he did nothing to help the canal financially. The state did not offer one dollar's aid. The reason was the powerful influence of the Hartford-based Connecticut River Company that opposed any competition to its dominance of Connecticut River traffic and was engaged in building a canal around the Enfield Rapids to allow navigation north of Hartford. Certainly, the lack of state money contributed to the project's failure.

Who would dig the big ditch? The staid Yankee Congregationalists were astonished when twenty-eight gangs of Irish immigrants, armed with picks and shovels, appeared along the proposed route. They labored in crews of ten to twenty each. Their heavy brogues, rough appearance, and limitless capacity of some for hard liquor caused consternation and resentment. When in 1832 a Catholic church was organized in New Haven, an editorial in the local paper was headed, "The Pope's Coming!" Needless to say, the Irish were not welcome; they were isolated and objects of distrust. Hired by contractors and subcontractors on the canal, they were the lowly, nameless diggers. Not only underpaid, the workers (as well as the contractors) were often paid late because of the company's teetering on insolvency. Sometimes, they were paid in script, redeemable at half the paper value.

A folk song the Irish crews loved to sing illustrated their harsh relationships with their employers:

> *A new foreman was Gene McCanna*
> *By God he was a blaming man.*
> *Last week a premature blast went off*
> *A mile in the air went Big Jim Croft.*
> *When next payday came around.*
> *Jim Croft was a dollar short. When he*
> *ask, "What for?" came the reply:*
> *"You were docked for the time*
> *You spent in the sky."*

By the summer of 1826, progress was visible in Farmington, although many residents were unhappy with the location of canal bridges and the construction of embankments. The dispute stopped further work for four months. The *Hartford Courant* made jibes at New Haven and the canal, calling it "the little ditch." By June 1828 a feeder canal began bringing water from the Farmington River and the aqueduct to carry the canal over the river were finished. In anticipation of the opening, the first canal boat, named the *James Hillhouse* in honor of the canal's superintendent, was launched. Two hundred ladies and gentlemen boarded the boat, which was drawn by three horses over the aqueduct.

The official opening, however, was delayed by heavy rain. On September 4, the embankment gave way and the mouth of the feeder canal damaged. By November all was repaired, and on November 10, the *James Hillhouse* left New Haven for Farmington carrying 60,000 shingles. Two days later, it rendezvoused in Farmington with the *Weatogue* coming south from Simsbury with a party of celebrants. The same afternoon, a packet boat from New Haven arrived with passengers and 100 barrels of salt. In the succeeding weeks the canal became busy with New Haven boats hauling commodities such as salt, sugar, molasses, flour, coffee, and hides; they returned with upcountry produce such as apples, cider, butter, and wood.

In 1835 the canal opened all the way to Northampton, Massachusetts. On July 30, the *Northampton,* using the Hampshire & Hampden Canal in Massachusetts and drawn by five horses at 4 miles per hour, completed the first through journey from Hillhouse Basin in New Haven to the Connecticut River. The 70-mile trip took twenty-four hours and cost passengers $3.75, including meals. It was greeted along the way by cheering crowds and a roaring cannon. When the last stretch was reached, four gray horses took the towline. From the bow of the *Northampton,* Governor Wolcott waved to the governor of Massachusetts. It seemed like an auspicious beginning.

But it was not to last. There were still long periods when the canal had to be closed because of breaks and the lack of income for adequate maintenance. Twice the big stone arch carrying it over Salmon Brook at Granby was washed away. In 1829 very dry weather impeded navigation; the next year, a bad break in the bank occurred, and that fall a drought forced closing a section for three months. Every time there was a break due to flooding, damages had to be paid to the farmers whose fields were inundated. Over a four-year period, the company spent over four times its total revenue. In the reorganization of 1836, the original investors lost $1 million.

In 1840 Joseph E. Sheffield of New Haven took control. Though still undercapitalized, the canal company did better; its

This photograph shows the Farmington Canal, near Mount Carmel in Hamden, between 1890 and 1909. CONNECTICUT HISTORICAL SOCIETY MUSEUM

best year, 1844, saw record-breaking tonnage, no days lost, and a good profit, the only one ever made. A severe drought the next July shut down the entire canal for two months.

Already a new and cheaper form of transportation was sealing the canal's doom, a steam-spouting iron monster that ran on tracks on dry land. Discouraged and fearful of a bleak future, the stockholders in 1846 accepted the inevitable and petitioned the legislature for the right to build a railroad. On January 11, 1848, the year trains began running from New Haven to Plainville, all canal operations ceased.

During the two decades of its existence, the Farmington Canal greatly stimulated the local economy. Agricultural output and manufactures could be easily and cheaply shipped and likewise imports brought in by merchants. Property values increased along the route. Farmington benefited by shipping wood to New Haven in its own line of boats. On Main Street the Union Hotel was, according to one young traveler, "an impressive sight." The number of retail stores jumped from twelve to eighteen. Plainville and Unionville also prospered. As the head of navigation because of the feeder dam and canal, Unionville was able to develop a flourishing industrial center. Recreation was another benefit: In winter there was skating on the canal and in summer swimming. These developments, however, could not obscure the fact that New Haven banks and individual investors had suffered heavy financial losses.

THE RESCUE OF KIDNAPPED AFRICANS

The *Amistad* Affair
1839

Connecticut played a bizarre yet significant role during the early antislavery movement in a legal struggle that went all the way to the Supreme Court. In the 1830s, although some Connecticut merchants were still clandestinely engaged in the slave trade, the ownership of slaves was not widespread in the state. Slaves were treated far more humanely than in the South, generally as household servants, farm workers, or tradespeople. The legislature had voted that slaves born after March 1, 1784, could not be held as servants after age twenty-six. Already, there was a rising antislavery movement: In Farmington, the Anti-Slavery Society had seventy male members (and forty women in its auxiliary), led by Noah Porter, the outspoken pastor of the First Congregational Church. One escaped slave, James W. C. Pennington, rose to become a prominent clergyman in Hartford and New Haven. Later, in 1848, Connecticut abolished slavery entirely.

The *Amistad* affair began in early 1839, when forty-nine young men, a boy, and three girls, most of them Mendi from what is now Sierra Leone, were kidnapped by fellow Africans and taken to the island of Lomboko off Africa's west coast. The Mendi had a proud, independent culture and had never been conquered. They lived a frugal life in small villages by growing rice. Both men and women participated in their government; even their judicial system was based on individual rights and included open-air trials.

On Lomboko a Spaniard named Pedro Blanco operated an infamous center of the transatlantic slave trade. Along with several hundred other blacks, the Mendi were crammed into the stifling hold of the Portuguese slave ship *Tecoro*. Poorly fed, routinely beaten, without sanitation, they were chained one to another in holds only 4 feet high. Many died on the long voyage to Havana, Cuba. By a treaty between Great Britain and Spain, such trade was illegal, but the lure of enormous profits enticed ship captains and traders to ignore the ban.

After the *Tecoro* reached Havana, they were herded into a barracoon or depot and on June 26, all were sold to two Spaniards, Jose Ruiz and Pedro Montes, who declared that the young Africans had arrived before the treaty and thus were slaves under Spanish law. The prisoners were loaded aboard the *Amistad,* a low, sleek schooner built in Baltimore as a slaver. In an ironic twist her Spanish name translated as "friendship." The following day, she set sail. Onboard, besides the prisoners, were two Spanish plantation owners, Captain Ferrer, his two mulatto slaves, and two white crewmen.

With favorable winds the voyage should not have taken more than two days, but the ship ran into strong headwinds under the intense tropical sun. Food and water were getting low. On the fourth day out, the captain's black cook taunted the captives by telling them that when they reached land, they would be killed and eaten by the plantation owners. Meanwhile, below deck the Africans had probably, in the Mendi tradition, chosen the twenty-five-year-old son of a Mendi chief as their leader. His name was Senghe Pieb; the Spanish called him Cinque. Intelligent and resourceful, he was determined to fight for their freedom. That night, Cinque and his accomplice Grabeau used a nail to pick the locks on the iron collars around their necks. After freeing the others, they found a shipment of machetes—sugar cane knives with 2-foot-long blades—and crept up onto the main deck in the rain-swept predawn hours of July 1. Killing the hated cook, they turned on the captain, who shot two of the Africans before being struck down. The two white sailors escaped in a boat. The two Spaniards, Ruiz and Montes, and the captain's personal slave, Antonio, were taken prisoners.

Within a few minutes Cinque had seized control of the schooner. Now he faced a much worse dilemma. He had only one goal in mind: to return to Africa. Though a farm boy ignorant of seafaring or navigation, he had observed that the *Tecora* had sailed toward the setting sun, so he reasoned the *Amistad* should be headed east toward the rising sun and ordered Montes to steer in that direction. No fool, Montes took advantage of darkness to change course to the northwest, hoping the schooner would encounter another vessel. Week after week the ship pursued a zigzag course along the East Coast of the United States; eight Africans perished from lack of food and water. The *Amistad* took on a ghostlike appearance as its sails became shredded. Other vessels avoided her when seeing the fierce-looking, heavily armed Africans manning the ship. They suspected she was a pirate.

This wood engraving depicts the death of Captain Ferrer when the captive passengers aboard the Amistad *armed themselves with cane knives and attacked.* CONNECTICUT HISTORICAL SOCIETY MUSEUM

Almost two months after the revolt, on August 26, Cinque had the ship anchored off the tip of Long Island and went ashore to barter for supplies. A naval warship, the USS *Washington,* under the command of Lt. Cdr. T. R. Gedney, appeared, quickly took control, and captured Cinque before he could row back. He tried to escape by leaping overboard. Hoping to earn a percentage of the value of both ship and human cargo, Gedney chose to tow his prize into New London.

Three days later, U.S. District Judge Andrew Judson held a hearing aboard the *Washington.* It was not a good omen. Six years earlier, he had headed the persecution of a Quaker, Prudence Crandall, for operating a school for black girls in Canterbury. Rather than submit to expelling the students, the courageous teacher closed her school and left Connecticut, never to return. Now Judson ordered the Mendi to be tried before the circuit court in Hartford for mutiny and murder. The captives were transferred to the New Haven jail to await trial in September. Already they had become public curiosities, as people paid twelve and a half cents for the privilege of filing through the jail to gawk at them. One visitor, John T. Norton of Farmington, wrote to a Hartford newspaper that "if these are fair specimens of native Africans, they are if possible more entitled to our sympathies and our benevolent efforts than I had supposed them to be."

In less than a week, the abolitionists had formed a committee to solicit funds for the prisoners' support and legal counsel. Its members were the Reverend Joshua Levitt, editor of a New York antislavery newspaper; the Reverend Simeon S. Jocelyn, a militant abolitionist New Haven clergyman who helped escaping slaves on their way to freedom via the underground railroad; and Lewis Tappan, a wealthy New York merchant. The prisoners were given food and warm clothing. The biggest problem for the defending attorneys was to overcome the language barrier. Luckily, they located in New York an African named John Ferry who spoke Mendi well enough to translate for them.

In mid-September the Africans arrived at the Connecticut State House in Hartford for a hearing before Justice Smith Thompson of the U.S. Supreme Court and the antiblack Judson. Thompson ruled that the Supreme Court had no jurisdiction to try the Africans because the *Amistad* was a Spanish ship, and the revolt had taken place in Spanish waters. The issue then for the circuit court boiled down to whether the prisoners were property or people with rights. Before the trial in November, the prisoners were allowed to live in New Haven. Desperate to improve communication so the Mendi could tell their full story, the defense turned to Josiah Willard Gibbs, a Yale professor, who learned the Mendi words for numbers 1 through 10 and then combed the New York docks repeating them outloud. In this way he found James Covey, a young Mendi who had learned English at a missionary school in Sierra Leone before becoming a British sailor.

Meanwhile, the case had become a diplomatic crisis with the Spanish and a political headache for U.S. President Martin Van Buren. The Spanish government, on the basis of previous treaties, demanded the return of the *Amistad* to her owners and the extradition of the Africans to Havana to stand trial. Eager to avoid an international incident and, equally important, not lose the support of southern Democrats in the impending 1840 presidential election (which he lost), Van Buren agreed to accept the Spanish demands. On the other hand, the abolitionists realized if the slaves were returned to Cuba, they would be put to death. They argued that the Africans were not *ladinos* (Spanish-speaking Africans, possibly from East Africa) being transported under Cuba's domestic slave trade but victims of the outlawed importation of slaves from Africa.

The trial opened on January 8, 1840, in New Haven. Several more of the captives had died, leaving only thirty-six. Anticipating a favorable verdict for the government, a ship had been stationed in New London to transport the hapless defendants back to Havana. After six days of dramatic testimony by Cinque and others, Judge Judson astonished the public by declaring they "were born free and ever since have been and still of right are free and not slaves." Commander Gedney was granted salvage rights on the ship. The district attorney, acting on orders from Washington, immediately appealed the decision.

More than a year elapsed before the Supreme Court heard the case, during which time public sympathy for the Africans' plight was aroused in numerous works of popular art, including a play called *The Black Schooner*, an exhibit of them in wax, and a painting of Cinque by Nathaniel Jocelyn that captured his great dignity, charisma, and strong will. New Haven historian

This engraving and mezzotint by John Sartain created ca. 1840 depicts Cinque, chief of the Amistad *captives. Cinque obtained his freedom and returned to his village in Africa—only to discover his wife and three children had been enslaved.*

John Warner Barber published a pamphlet with a hand-colored engraving depicting the shipboard revolt. For the first time, each survivor was seen as a human being with a life and family from which he been forcibly separated.

Still, the odds were stacked against freedom, since five of the judges were Southerners unlikely to be sympathetic. A champion of national stature was needed. The abolitionists finally chose "Old Man Eloquent," as the seventy-three-year-old John Quincy Adams was affectionately known near the end of his distinguished career as a lawyer, minister to Russia and England, secretary of state, senator, and president (from 1824 to 1828). In 1830 he was elected to Congress. A popular critic of the Democrats but not an abolitionist, he favored gradual emancipation through constitutional amendments. He teamed up with Roger Sherman Baldwin of New Haven (elected governor in 1844), who reviewed the basic facts: The Africans had never been slaves under Spanish law, their action to free themselves was not a crime, and the federal government's interference was inappropriate and illegal. When his turn came, the often imperious Adams passionately attacked the Van Buren administration for its shameful interference, stressed the Africans' search for justice, and compared their revolt with those heroes who had overthrown tyrants in ancient Athens. On March 9, the court completely vindicated the defendants and released them from custody. "Glorious," exulted Roger Baldwin. "Glorious not only as a triumph of humanity and justice, but as a vindication of our national character from reproach and dishonor."

What would happen now? Where would the freed slaves go? The citizens of Farmington, led by Sam Deming, Austin Williams, and John T. Norton, came to the rescue. There they could continue their education and perhaps be converted to Christianity to serve as missionaries in their home country. After they arrived by train and sleigh, shivering under buffalo robes, a special building was erected for the men and boy. The three girls were housed in private homes. At first the reaction of the village was mixed; some residents feared they might be murdered in their beds, but gradually the opposition subsided except for occasional friction. The men pursued a daily schedule of farmwork and craft work, formal schooling, and instruction in Christianity. One girl, Kali, sent John Q. Adams a Bible in appreciation.

As welcomed as they were, the freed Africans yearned to go home; one became so depressed he drowned himself in the turbulent Farmington River. Funds were raised in part by showing them off at antislavery meetings. At long last on November 17, a farewell ceremony was held at the church attended by representatives from fourteen towns and several hundred residents. Hymns were sung. An additional $1,300 more was raised. At 5:00 the next morning, a crowd gathered to see them off on the canal boat. Tears flowed as the Africans embraced their friends. Accompanied by several young missionaries and their wives, they set sail from New York and fifty-two days later reached the port of Freetown in Sierra Leone in January 1842. The men scattered to their villages. One of the girls, Margru, later went back to America to study at Oberlin College in Ohio, the first college to admit black students.

For Cinque it was not a happy reunion. He discovered his wife and three children had been captured and sold into slavery. He left the mission in Sierra Leone to trade down the coast. At the end of his life, in 1879, he suddenly reappeared outside the mission and announced he had come to die. Within a week he was dead.

In 1989 the poignant story of the *Amistad* was retold by the New Haven Colony Historical Society and the Connecticut Historical Society in an impressive exhibit. Steven Spielberg's feature film *Amistad* was released in 1997. This in turn inspired Mystic Seaport to build a replica of the schooner, launched in March 2000 to cruise Long Island Sound and the East Coast as a floating classroom.

BRIDGE OUT!

The Norwalk Train Wreck

1853

The era of steam transportation progressed from waterborne ships to land-based trains in less than twenty years. In 1832 the Connecticut legislature chartered the New York and Stonington Railroad to construct a railroad in Stonington that would run to Providence and thence to Boston. This eliminated the need for steamboats to reach Providence by rounding stormy Point Judith, frequently a disagreeable passage for passengers with queasy stomachs. The railroad proved to be the first great industry: From fewer than 50 miles of track in 1837 by the 1890s there were more than 1,000. A local historian, Ellen Larned, captured the railroad's impact upon the Connecticut economy when she wrote in 1880: "Windham County dates its birth from the first whistle of the steam engine. That clarion cry awoke the sleeping valleys. . . . At every stopping place new life sprung up." The trains made up for the state's notorious dirt roads and served as a catalyst for the development of its dominance in manufacturing textiles, munitions, brass, silver, and hardware.

Christmas Day in 1848 saw the first sign of Connecticut's extensive railroad system when another line, the New York & New Haven, planned to run its first train. The track had not been completed as scheduled, and the flag-draped train with its load of celebrants had to back up on the single track to the New Haven station. Soon the line was open all the way to New York; a week before the inaugural run the *Stamford Advocate* observed its trial trip:

> The citizens of the village, as well as horses and cattle, were nearly frightened out of their propriety by such a horrible scream as was never heard to issue from other than a metallic throat. Animals of every description went careening around the fields, snuffing at the air in their terror. In a few moments the cause of the commotion appeared in the shape of a locomotive, puffing off its steam and screaming with its so-called whistle at a terrible rate.

The line was profitable from the start. Fares were $1.50. In the 1850s a second track was started to handle the traffic. By 1855 there were 26 engines, 80 wooden coaches, and more than 300 freight cars in service.

At 8 A.M. on May 6, 1853, Dr. Gurdon Wadsworth Russell of Hartford and other physicians, with considerable excitement, boarded a fast new train in Manhattan, the most recent to serve the route from New York to Boston. They were returning from the three-day annual meeting of the American Medical Association. Thirty-eight-year-old Dr. Russell, a graduate of Yale Medical School, was now medical director of the Aetna Life Insurance Company. The train was jammed with 150 passengers.

MAY 21, 1853.]   ILLUSTRATED NEWS.   333

THE LATE RAILWAY CALAMITY AT NORWALK, CONN.

Leslie's Illustrated News *depicted the New York & New Haven rail catastrophe*
with this dramatic wood engraving, published May 21, 1853.
CONNECTICUT HISTORICAL SOCIETY MUSEUM

At 10:15 A.M. Captain Byxbie of the steamboat *Pacific* filled
with passengers whistled for passage through the draw at South
Norwalk, 300 yards east of the station. The draw was a wooden
span that pivoted on a central pier, creating two 60-foot openings. The rail line ran across the span at about 25 feet above
water. On this morning the tide was high, reaching a depth of
12 feet. The bridge tender, Mr. Harford, listened to make sure
no train was coming from either direction, and hearing none,
he lowered the 2-foot red ball sitting atop a 40-foot pole, and
then opened the bridge to vessels. (If the ball had been up, as
the engineer later claimed, it would have incorrectly signaled

the soon-to-be-arriving Boston express that the bridge was closed to vessels, thus causing the disaster.) The steamboat passed through. As Harford was just about to close the span, at about 10:30 A.M., he was horrified to see the 8:00 express to Boston round the curve at 25 miles per hour and plunge into the river. Its speed carried the engine clear across the western channel against the central pier. A baggage car, two mail cars, and two passenger cars followed, while a third car was left suspended over the brink of the draw and broke in half.

Almost forty victims in the first two passenger cars drowned; a crew from the steamboat rescued others by pulling them from the water. Seven of the dead were Dr. Wadsworth's fellow doctors, including Dr. Archibald Welch of Wethersfield, who at the time was president of the Connecticut Medical Society. The three-man train crew saved themselves by jumping—the engineer Edward Tucker (who was a substitute) breaking his leg, the fireman Ellman uninjured, and the conductor Charles H. Comstock only bruised. A crowd gathered, turned against the crew, and urged that the engineer be executed on the spot, opinion differing only as to method—hanging or shooting!

As soon as he got home, Dr. Russell was asked by the *Hartford Courant* to write his account of the accident, probably the first eyewitness description by a physician of such a disaster. His account appeared on May 7.

> The first thing I noticed was a waving and jerking of the cars . . . enough to show that an accident of some kind had occurred. It was so different, however, from what I had supposed to be the case when cars are off from the track that I thought they would be stopped and that we were safe. This

was but for a moment, for the breaking of the glass and of the car showed that something terrible had happened or was about to happen, for at this time I supposed that the one we occupied [the last car] was the only car injured. There came then a shaking and a crash and a stop, and in a moment the work was done. The front of the car and part of the floor had broken off just in front of me, one end resting on the bridge and the other on the cars in the water below. So sudden and rapid was the whole affair that we had but time for a moment's thought, and it was over. Helping up those on the inclined floor, who were not seriously injured, we next went down to those in the water. . . . It was evident that here were two cars full of passengers, and one had fallen on top of the other; the upper one was inclined on its side and nearly filled with water. We immediately commenced taking out the inmates at the windows, and soon got out a large number, some injured, some bruised, and many, ah, far too many, dead.

These were, apparently, not killed in the majority of instances by bruises or severe blows, but presented all the symptoms of asphyxia from drowning, and were probably drowned at once, being confined and pressed by broken cars.

The shrieks of the terrified women and children, the supplications of those in the water below . . . formed a scene . . . which can never be forgotten . . . My narrow escape was pressed home on me more closely when I recognized among the dead him for whom I had given up my seat in New York and had taken the succeeding car.

There was an inquest into the disaster that held the engineer, Tucker, primarily responsible through gross negligence.

He insisted he had seen the red ball aloft before approaching the bridge, but other witnesses—including the bridge tender, steamboat captain, and passersby—testified that the red ball had been lowered well before the train came around the final curve. The ball, it was proven, could first be seen by eastbound trains at a distance of 3,300 feet. Two years after the tragedy, the New York & New Haven settled death claims in an amount estimated at $290,000.

Dr. Russell continued as Aetna's medical director until 1902. During his half century in that position, he pioneered the field of life insurance medicine and underwriting. He died in 1909 at the age of ninety-four.

THAT DEMON, STEAM!

The Fales & Gray Explosion

1854

In its early industrial history, Connecticut's most abundant natural resource was water. The Connecticut River served as a highway for maritime trade along the East Coast, to the West Indies, and as far away as China. Other rivers and streams provided the waterpower for operating the local gristmills, sawmills, and fulling mills. In fact the availability of water determined the location of most mills and shops, as well as the villages founded around them, until well into the nineteenth century. America's first great engineer, Oliver Evans, developed the high-pressure steam engine that enabled industry to convert from waterpower to steam power; its first use in Connecticut was in a Middletown woolen mill in 1811. Without steam the Colt Armory could never have run at all, but steam was always regarded with a great respect and even fear. For steam could be a demon.

By 1850, as Sam Colt started to plan his Armory, steam power had become as common as the horse and buggy, pushing sidewheelers up and down the Connecticut River, moving trains on spreading networks of tracks, and running machines. In Hartford shops thirty engines of various sizes panted and heaved. In many eyes, however, stationary as it might seem, a steam engine was an occult force that spewed forth a hot, white breath, a monster that on occasion men were helpless to control. Few understood how steam worked. Explosions occurred with alarming regularity—in the entire country as frequently as once or twice a week. Thousands had lost their lives. But these explosions were all considered "acts of God" caused by "mysterious agencies," static electricity, or a combination of gases.

Colt's engine was the biggest of all—250 horsepower. Built by Woodruff & Beach in Hartford, it had a 3-foot cylinder and 7-foot stroke, with a flywheel 30 feet in diameter. Two large boilers supplied the steam. A leather belt over 100 feet long carried the power to the attic and thence to the 1,400 machines by means of an intricate network of overhead shafts and smaller belts. To start up in the morning, the engineer had to light his fire two hours before the 7 A.M. gong, signaling the beginning of the workday. The buildings themselves were steam-heated through pipes running along the walls. Gas burners supplied light. The same engine also operated a cam pump that raised water from the Connecticut River to a reservoir that supplied both the Armory and its surrounding dwellings. Later, another engine—almost twice as powerful—was installed.

A few blocks from Colt's, near the waterfront, stood the Fales & Gray Car Works, builders of railroad cars. In the blacksmith shop iron was annealed in white-hot furnaces and hammered into various shapes by sooty smiths and their helpers, called strikers. Next to the shop, separated by an 8-inch-thick wall of brick, were the boiler room and steam engine, only one-fifth as powerful as Colt's.

Its operator was John McCune, an easygoing but temperamental young man, who, although not yet thirty, had been firing boilers for nine years. He was generally regarded as competent, no better and no worse that his counterparts in other manufacturing establishments. He had received no professional training—in fact, like other stationary engineers his education was minimal, and he had learned his trade on the job.

For quite a while the blacksmiths had been uneasy about the old boiler and their proximity to it. Its two flues could barely get up enough steam to keep the machines operating. The boss was doubtless on McCune's neck every day for more pressure. But the boiler leaked, and the only way McCune could do his job was to cheat. He hung lead weights on the safety valve. If Fales or Gray noticed, they never said a word. But the blacksmiths were not blind.

Some of the workers also suspected that McCune drank too much. Downing a beer or two during the dinner hour at the Front Street saloon was no crime, and on Saturday night a man might be expected to take a few too many and stagger home. But if an engineer returned from dinner drunk, he might forget to keep the water level up in the boiler. McCune was headstrong and surly if crossed, and there were rumors of trouble within his family. Not that he beat his wife, but his neighbors couldn't help overhearing the verbal warfare that rattled the walls of his Pearl Street home.

These concerns about the boiler and McCune were passed off as jokes. They never reached management's ears. No one dared to complain or squeal. So they remained silent about their shared fear: that a leaky boiler, overpressured and perhaps neglected now and then, could send them all into the next world without time enough for even a "Hail, Mary."

Six months before, McCune had quit his job. He told his boss the boiler was no good; he was overworked and needed a second fireman to help load the coal. His replacement was a failure. The company recalled McCune, giving him a raise from $1.50 to $1.75 a day, another helper, and a special favor. Unlike the rest of the workforce, he could collect his wages every Saturday night. Furthermore, the company promised to order a new boiler, with five flues, from Woodruff & Beach, the best boiler- and engine makers in Hartford and suppliers to factories all over Connecticut.

The new boiler had been in operation about a month when it happened. Thursday, March 2, 1854, was an unseasonably warm day. As if ending a winter of hibernation, people emerged from their houses and tenements to enjoy the sun. After a leisurely dinner, William Skinner, a local printer, strolled past the blacksmith shop, delaying as long as possible his return to work. A friend rapped on the window and invited him inside, though it was against company rules to admit visitors. It was 1:45 P.M. The engine was pounding away as usual, the wheels overhead turning smoothly, and the anvils ringing with rhythmic hammer blows. After chatting a few minutes, Skinner headed for the door through the boiler room. He stopped to talk with the engineer, whom he knew slightly. As he departed through the door, a tremendous explosion shook the factory, breaking timbers, mangling machinery and men, knocking down walls for 100 feet, and collapsing the roof. The blacksmith shop and the boiler room were completely demolished. Nine men were killed at once; twelve more died later. Fifty were seriously injured.

McCune's body was hurled through the boiler room door and landed, minus one arm, next to William Skinner. Skinner was flattened, his left arm broken, his neck scalded, and his head cut. Two men were blown through the shop windows. A falling timber crushed Samuel Parsons at his lathe, but he was pulled out alive. Alex Nodine was sitting on the toilet on the second floor. The force of the explosion lifted him 10 feet into the air, and as the floor under him gave way, he fell to the floor below, with only his head gashed.

Within minutes a crowd gathered at the scene of destruction. Hysterical wives and their children searched for their husbands. Some soon realized they were widows and orphans. So great was the excitement that the South District School was dismissed for the afternoon. Before dark the injured and dead were removed, and a coroner's jury of twelve leading business and professional men summoned. It was the worst calamity in Hartford's history.

At 10:00 the next morning, the jury, after inspecting the site and the remains of the boiler, convened for the investigation. For six days they heard testimony under oath from workers, managers, the boiler manufacturer, consultants, and others. The first witness was Patrick Munhall, the twenty-five-year-old fireman who was McCune's assistant. A minute or two before the explosion, he had told McCune either he had too much steam on or the water was low, and then went into the cellar for more coal, thus saving his life.

Around two P.M. I asked McCune, "Is there water in the boiler?" and he replied, "I'm just taking water on from the pump." I warned him the gauge was up to 82, and he ought to take down the damper. McCune said not to worry, everything was all right. I don't know if he did anything about the water or the damper.

A high-pressure steam boiler of this kind had a rated safe operating limit of about 50–60 pounds of pressure per square inch. Munhall and others confirmed that it was customary to push it up to 80 pounds or higher, otherwise all the machines couldn't be kept running. At 88 pounds per square inch, the pressure on the entire boiler would equal 4,320,000 pounds.

Daniel Duffy was the next witness. He had looked after the boiler while the engineer went out for dinner at noontime. Under questioning he admitted that he knew McCune drank, but he had never seen him drunk. The foreman of the machine shop, Gordon Grant, opened up another line of investigation:

> Sometimes I thought McCune was careless in letting the water get low, and I used to speak to him about it. He'd say the new boiler made steam very fast but he wasn't concerned at all. No, the water pump was not out of order. It's my business to repair it.

Grant said in his opinion McCune was always sober at work, although he knew he drank outside. "But he wasn't much of an engineer. Sometimes he'd have the steam up as high as 95, and sometimes he'd allow the water in the flues to drop below the lowest gauge cock." George Stone, a machinist, agreed with Grant that the engineer was occasionally sloppy, yet he considered him as good as other engineers he knew.

Seth King testified that shortly after the dinner hour he had seen McCune talking with the visitor Skinner. According to him Skinner and McCune conversed for about fifteen minutes

When the boiler exploded at Fales & Gray, it was not the leaky old boiler that did the damage but a new one that had been in operation for about a month. CONNECTICUT HISTORICAL SOCIETY MUSEUM

near the door of the boiler room. When he finished, the jurors looked at each other, eyebrows raised.

The jury than called Thomas J. Fales, thirty-eight, the proprietor. Fales had been at dinner when the disaster occurred. He reviewed McCune's employment record over the preceding five years. "After two or three years here he became slovenly in the care of the engine. I reproved him, and he did better. He liked the new boiler and often said 'see how easy I can now get up steam enough.'"

Question: Wasn't it dangerous to operate the boiler at 80 pounds pressure or higher?

Fales: No, sir, that boiler would be safe at 150. It was made of the best iron and had extra thick plates.

Question: Did you have any reason to believe McCune was careless?

Fales: Well, as I have said, he was sometimes sloppy— he didn't keep the room clean. But I always thought him a reliable worker . . . never heard any complaint about his being careless. Of course, if he was talking to Skinner, it was wrong. We don't allow that sort of thing.

Question: Did you ride him about keeping the pressure up?

Fales: He had orders to produce sufficient power, but I warned him against doing anything rash or unsafe.

Question: Did you suspect McCune ever drank too much?

Fales: No, sir. I never heard that said about him. Once I had to bawl him out . . . I think it was last summer . . . for leaving his engine to get a glass of beer. But nobody ever mentioned to me that he was intemperate or careless.

From George Balmer, McCune's father-in-law, the jury tried to find out more about the engineer's personal life, without success. All that Balmer would admit was that many husbands and fathers were more agreeable at home that John McCune. Dr. David Crary, the family physician, knew of McCune's drinking habits and had urged him to leave the stuff alone. "But I never could get him to promise he would stop."

John Cook, a fifty-year-old mason, was full of bitterness:

I told somebody this boiler'd blow up in six weeks. John had been used to attending a boiler with two flues, and this one had five, and he would get a little careless, and the water would get down before he was aware of it. "Watch out," I said. All he said was, "I can manage."

The jury by now had a pretty good lead on the cause of the explosion, but they still wanted to interview two witnesses, Charles Gardner and William Skinner, who had been so badly injured they were unable to attend the hearing. They also wanted to determine the safety of the boiler itself. They called Samuel Woodruff, president of Woodruff & Beach, builders of engines for Colt's, the Hartford Water Works, and the U.S. Navy.

Woodruff insisted the boiler had been built especially for the heavy demands that would be put on it. "We never turned out a better boiler than that one. It was full able to sustain a pressure of 88 pounds. If it had plenty of water, it would have borne a pressure of 150 pounds without bursting." Woodruff, however, was critical of the engineer and the trade in general. McCune never should have left his boiler and engine even for a minute. Furthermore, there ought to be a board to examine operating engineers and license them, and boilers should be regularly inspected, just like steamboat boilers.

Edward Reed, superintendent of the Hartford & New Haven Railroad Company, called up as a consultant, conceded he had no reservations about the boiler being well made. But he chose his words carefully when talking about its operation.

There is evidence, however, that the boiler was out of water. I examined the flues, and inside they were blue. Now, blueness denotes that they had been subjected to a red heat. In my opinion the accident was caused by a lack of water in the boiler, and steam was generated faster than it could escape. The boiler would not be unsafe even at 88 pounds if it were full of water.

The last expert to testify was Samuel Ward, a steamboat inspector. He took issue with Woodruff and Reed on the question of the boiler's safety limits. In his opinion, 80 to 90 pounds of pressure was too much. Then he roundly condemned those who call themselves boiler engineers.

Seven-eighths of these damn engineers are incompetent. They can only build a fire and start an engine. To show their daring, they attach extra weights to the safety valves. They know nothing about the dangers. What they do is criminal!

To complete the testimony depositions were taken from Gardner and Skinner. Gardner was only twenty years old, a striker in the blacksmith shop, who had his leg broken and his body burned. His account made quite an impression on the jury.

Two or three minutes before the explosion I saw McCune start the pump. He usually ran it every fifteen minutes or so. But sometimes he'd forget. I've seen the safety valve blow off steam a half dozen times. I've seen him away from the boiler so long the fireman had to go and start the pump. That very morning I told him, "if that thing blows up, it'll kill me and a lot more," He said he didn't like five flues, they worked his water off too fast, and he was always tired out at the end of the day. "God," he said, "I'll have a blow up if I'm not more careful, I guess."

William Skinner did his best to counteract the previous testimony so damaging to McCune's reputation.

When I reached the boiler room, the engineer urged me to sit down. Daniel Camp came up. "Come, Bill," he said, "can't you afford to give us a glass of beer, John and I?" But McCune declined: "No gentlemen, I can't leave my engine, you must excuse me." Camp then headed for the blacksmith shop, and McCune returned to his boiler. We were only together for five . . . no more than eight . . . minutes.

But it was to no avail. Otis Long, a blacksmith, described how the water pump had suddenly stopped after McCune's last start-up.

I was just picking up an iron, my striker had struck two blows, and as I turned to the fire I was blown down. Just before the blow up I heard a funny noise. The pump started up all right, then it hissed and stopped. The noise seemed to come from the pump's steam cylinder. I know that the pump had not run a half hour before dinner and during the hour after dinner.

Finally, the jury produced a surprise witness, a painter named John Proffitt, who lived next door to McCune.

Question: Did you accompany John McCune home to dinner on the day of the explosion?
Proffitt: I did.

Question: Did both of you stop on the way?

Proffitt: Yes, we did.

Question: Where?

Proffitt: At the saloon. We had a few drinks.

Question: What did you drink?

Proffitt: Well, I had an ale or two. John drank ale or
             brandy, or maybe both, I forget.

The hearing ended on that note. The jury promptly concluded that the explosion was due to the carelessness and inat-
tention of John McCune to an abnormally high steam pressure
and to the sudden injection of cold water, which collapsed the
red-hot flues. It also chided the company for not locating the
boiler room in a separate building away from the employees.

The jury was not content merely to establish blame. It sug-
gested several ways to prevent a recurrence of this and similar
tragedies. There should be regulations preventing unqualified
persons from being hired as operating engineers. There
should be regular safety inspections by the city or state.
Employers should pay heed to worker safety and isolate boiler
rooms. And there should be standards set for steam pressure.

Hartford was in no mood to write *finis* to the case after the
jury adjourned. For the relief of those injured or bereaved, a
collection was taken up in the city. The men at Rogers Brothers gave $153. Amos Whitney, then a foreman at Phoenix Iron
Works, raised $113 in his shop, and Wyatt's Dramatic Lyceum
collected $150 from its patrons. Altogether contributions
amounted to $8,100.

The city council was moved to appoint a committee to
study steam boiler safety, but like most committees it produced
no concrete results. Ten years would pass before the state leg-

islature enacted a boiler inspection law. A more immediate result came from a public meeting to discuss the city's lack of medical facilities. Well-to-do citizens were outraged that those injured in the explosion could be cared for only in nearby homes or in overcrowded doctor's offices. Before the end of May, Hartford's first public hospital was chartered; it offered free medical and surgical care until 1892.

The clergy had their say, too. From the pulpits of at least two churches, they made a moral issue of the disaster. The *Hartford Courant* printed the sermons, and in response to a heavy demand, made reprints and sold them for two cents apiece.

Thomas Clark, rector of Christ Church, had as inspiration for his text, I Samuel 20:3: "There is but a step between me and death." In his view mechanical power in the rapidly changing world around him was a mighty, mysterious force whose strength seemed to increase as it reached toward the spiritual, unknown realm. The import of his sermon eluded most of his parishioners. Did he mean that only God understood and had mastery of steam power? But his conclusion, that suffering was in some way essential to our permanent good, made them feel better for having attended the service.

Frederic Hinckley, pastor of the Church of the Saviour, delivered a down-to-earth inflammatory discourse entitled, "Where Is Abel Thy Brother?", taken from Genesis 4:9. Abel, of course, was dead, and the culprit was not only the imprudent engineer but also a pernicious attitude common to the captains of industry. The men who died, he told his aroused audience, were

sacrificed to the reckless spirit of enterprise of this mid-century; uselessly, murderously destroyed that more physical power might be obtained, more speed secured, more work performed, and greater material results produced. . . . Life is thus turned into a race between power and speed on the one hand, and human safety and human existence on the other.

The Fales & Gray management naturally interpreted this diatribe as an accusation of their personal guilt, and Mr. Fales wasted no time in issuing a flat denial that he pushed or drove his work force beyond the proper limits of safety. Then he neatly turned the tables on the Reverend Hinckley.

In a letter to the local paper, Fales wrote as follows:

Hardly three months ago one of your servants was burned to death upon your very hearthstone. . . . Such accidents are much more frequent in this community than steam boiler explosions. Very few of those who go to church have to do in any way with the management of steam engines and boilers, while there is scarcely a congregation in this state which does not contain a score of people who nightly use burning fluids or camphene, without comprehending the principles, as utterly ignorant as was your unfortunate servant.

Suppose some clergyman of this city charged the guilt of this woman's awful death upon you? Sacrificed, perhaps he would have said, uselessly, murderously destroyed that a cheaper light might be obtained for the use of a single family. The immediate cause of this deplorable accident, he might have continued, was the carelessness of the girl herself. But in this, as in most other instances, that cause did not stand alone. And, then, in tones of solemn severity he might have accused you before the public of culpable neglect, of sinful careless-ness, in permitting her to use this dangerous stuff.

Subsequently, Edward Reed, superintendent of the Hartford & New Haven Railroad Company, who had testified at the hearing, and a number of younger businessmen formed the Polytechnic Club to discuss "matters of science in relation to everyday life." It was natural that steam power would be their favorite topic. They wondered how boiler explosions could best be prevented and logically concluded that an inspection and insurance company, modeled after a similar experiment in England, was both a desirable and feasible solution. Nothing happened, however, until after the Civil War, by which time Hartford, with more than a dozen fire, life, and marine insurance companies flourishing, already had the reputation of being the "Insurance City." In 1866 the Hartford Steam Boiler Inspection & Insurance Company was organized, and among the first directors were Charles M. Beach, who had served as a juror on the coroner's panel, and the president of Colt's, Richard Jarvis.

The event helped to elect Morgan Bulkeley mayor in 1880. At the same time, fully conscious of the future of electricity as a source of power, he laid the groundwork for creating a public utility to supply it. Despite opposition from the Gas Company and two other petitioners, the Hartford Electric Light Company was granted a charter by the state legislature in 1881. Austin Dunham became president. At first the city's common council was hostile to the electrification of street lights, condemning poles as ugly and overhead wires as hazardous. The Gas Company, to protect its investment in municipal lighting, used its political clout to delay a decision as long as possible. In 1884 a contract was finally approved, and within four years the last gas lamp had been replaced, making Hartford the first city to have electric street lighting.

GUNS BLAZING

The Colt Armory Fire
1864

When in 1855 the famous gunmaker Samuel Colt completed building his factory in Hartford's South Meadows, it was the largest private armory in the world, and Colt made his fortune in less than fourteen years. Most of his life had been a failure, both at school and in business. Now this inventor, pitchman, and self-promoter was earning enormous profits as the North and South raced toward the Civil War; he was filling the demands of both sides for what he sardonically called "my latest work on Moral Reform."

Under the supervision of Colt's able superintendent, Elisha K. Root, the Armory mass produced the parts for the guns. Root invented much of the machinery in operation. Most of the 1,700 workers on two ten-hour shifts were the employees of twenty-five contractors who specialized in machining, filing, forging, rifling, polishing, and cartridge making. By 1860 Colt's had produced more than 300,000 revolvers.

The Armory, built of Portland brownstone with a slate roof, was 500 feet long by 60 feet wide, three stories high, and had a wing extending east from the center by 250 feet. On top of the Armory, Colt raised an onion-shaped blue dome, supported by columns and crowned by a golden sphere on which perched a rampant colt holding a broken spear. Showmanship at its ostentatious best, the dome proclaimed to the world Colt's great achievement—though he lived only seven years more to enjoy his fame. Worn out, he died at the age of forty-seven in January 1862, the country's first manufacturing tycoon. Before his death Colt had anticipated the army's need for even more muskets and revolvers, and he doubled the size of the Armory. At a cost of $1 million, the new South Armory was joined to the original East Armory.

But within two years a catastrophe almost put an end to his empire. It happened in the East Armory on a Friday in early February 1864.

Shortly after 8 A.M. the deep tones of the Colt steam gong sounded the alarm. Smoke was discovered emanating from the wing of the main brownstone building over the polishing room. The fire seemed centered in the attic near the main driving pulley for the machines. Men carried hose to the location, but there was no water. In minutes, all the upper stories were aflame. The top floor, laden with wooden patterns, collapsed. The workmen below who, according to plant custom, were locked into their departments, grew panicky until released. The fire now raced along faster than they could run, intensifying as it consumed the oil-soaked floors. A few escaped by the windows with their hair ablaze. With a terrible fury, flames shot through the aisles and doors amid the crash of falling timbers.

Like a tempestuous sea of fire, the flames rolled up into the sky and mixed with clouds of black smoke that hung over the city like a pall. Thousands hurried to the scene. Volunteer fire companies arrived with their newly acquired steamers and laid out 700 feet of hoses from the river to the blazing building. Again and again the hoses burst. Soon Mrs. Colt herself stood in front of the spellbound onlookers, accompanied by her father, a retired minister. At 9 A.M. the beautiful Colt dome teetered. With its glittering stars on a blue background, it looked like a huge balloon suspended in the air. As it fell, Mrs. Colt burst into tears, its collapse feeling like a second funeral for her husband.

Within half an hour the entire front of the Armory was a mass of rolling, surging flame, the roar mingled with the shouts of firemen, the crashing of woodwork, and the ceaseless wail of the steam gong. A drunk, wearing a fireman's hat and carrying a trumpet, climbed the office roof and pointed a rifle at the crowd. There was some pistol stealing, and one contingent of firemen found a hoard of liquor in the office cellar, disabling them for the rest of the day. An explosion of powder forced the mob back to escape the intense heat.

The floors of yellow pine had been thoroughly saturated with oil dripping from the machinery. In the attic, where the fire originated, a large number of wooden patterns burned quickly. Cracking and snapping, the flames shot through with terrible fury; timbers fell here and there; the black smoke curled in the air. Working its way north, the fire raced through the covered bridge to the company's brick office 30 feet distant.

Both the police and fire departments met with frustrating problems. Policemen were busy keeping the crowd of onlookers at a safe distance and arresting several would-be looters. The Stillman Hose Company, using old hand pumpers, assisted by a bucket brigade of workmen and volunteers, found Colt's reservoirs inadequate, forcing them to take three of their four "steamers" to the river and attach 750 feet of hose to each

In 1864 a mysterious fire destroyed the Colt Armory beyond recognition.
CONNECTICUT HISTORICAL SOCIETY MUSEUM

pumper. The hoses burst repeatedly. None the less, considerable property was removed to safety.

The other factories in the city engaged in war work—Sharps Rifle Company, Woodruff & Beach (boilermakers), George S. Lincoln (machine tools), and Pratt & Whitney—shut down so that their employees could render assistance. With their help Colt's saved the new armory, the brick walls of which made it more fire resistant. Thus, production of muskets continued without interruption.

But the company's office was destroyed, as were most of Root's machinery and a quantity of finished revolvers, as well as all the drawings and models. Silenced too were the giant steam engines.

Amazingly, only one man perished. Edwin K. Fox, about fifty years old and the father of six children, had been in and out of the building several times helping to remove property. The last time he entered with his boss Joseph Williams, seeing the flames making rapid headway, Williams started to leave and called Fox to follow. But Fox didn't, the roof collapsed, and he was burned to death. Another employee, Amesa Colburn, was struck by a falling timber and badly burned.

All day Saturday and Sunday, people flocked to gaze upon the destruction. Fifteen hundred feet of crumbling masonry stretched around broken stone and white-heated iron. A Colt executive, possibly Horace Lord, Root's successor and superintendent, gazed forlornly at the desolation and said, "If any one had to come to us yesterday and offered us 4 million for what is destroyed, we wouldn't have looked at it!"

It was one of the worst calamities ever to befall a Hartford industry. Nine hundred men thrown out of work just when their labor was most needed! A few pails of water in the attic might have held the fire in check. One thousand lathes and millers laid in ruin on the ground, surrounded by crumbled masonry and twisted iron. Altogether, the damage exceeded $1,250,000. During his lifetime Colonel Colt had disdained buying insurance, believing his works were fireproof. His successor, having a different outlook, had recently covered part of the buildings and their contents, so that Colt's was able to recover about a third of the total loss.

On Sunday, the Reverend Bernard Peters preached a sermon based on verses from Job—"yet man is born into trouble, as the sparks fly upward." As the embers cooled, crowds continued to gather all weekend to see the devastation. The press called for a paid fire department with each steamer drawn by two horses instead of by human volunteers. Lydia Sigourney, Hartford's sweet poetess, penned a suitable condolence, as she did for every bereavement. Prescott and Gage, a local photographer, offered the public pictures of the ruins, while the city speculated on the cause of the conflagration. Some blamed it on friction from the pulley in the attic. President Root disproved this theory pointing out that the gearing for the pulley was encased in heavy iron boxes. Others laid it to the combustible pistol stocks stored in the attic drying room or to cotton waste left by a careless handyman after oiling the pulley. Mrs. Colt and several Colt contractors suspected sabotage, possibly the work of Jefferson Davis's secret agents. The final answer was never determined.

What would happen to the armory? Elizabeth Colt did not hesitate a day. She ordered it rebuilt exactly as her husband left it, no matter how much the cost. City officials also acted quickly, establishing a paid fire service in October. But the rebuilding of the armory took several years. The end of the war removed any sense of urgency. Nothing was started until a retired major general joined Colt's as vice president and general manager in November 1865, a few months after President Root's death. Mrs. Colt's brother, Richard Jarvis, now headed the company. The new executive, William B. Franklin, had been trained as an engineer, graduating from West Point in the same class as General Grant.

Franklin wasted no time in carrying out the widow's wishes. On November 20, he wrote in his diary:

Examined roof of the New Armory building with reference
to rebuilding the burnt part. Found New Armory had settled
a great deal. Resolved to pile the foundations for the
columns. Talked with Mr. Lord about increasing production
of pistols.

By February of the following year, he had designed the new
structure, estimated its cost at $130,000 exclusive of machin-
ery, and obtained approval from the directors. It was decided to
make it four stories and as fireproof as possible. Meanwhile, as
a safety measure, Horace Lord, the superintendent, was
instructed to set up a fire brigade in each story of the existing
buildings and to place the hoses on reels. The foundations
were laid in April and the work was finished in early 1867,
including a new dome.

AN ICY PLUNGE

The Tariffville Bridge Wreck

1878

On the cold afternoon of January 15, 1878, a special ten-car train drawn by two engines of the seven-year-old Connecticut Western Railroad puffed out of the Simsbury Station headed for Hartford, a distance of 15 miles. It was jammed with 200 followers of the charismatic Dwight L. Moody, the Boston evangelist, who that evening would hold a revival meeting. The most famous Protestant leader of his time, Moody preached the old-time gospel in partnership with David Sankey, singer and organist. The meeting was a great success, and those who had come from the western towns trudged joyfully back to Union Station for the return trip.

The train with two engines left about 9:20 P.M. and stopped briefly at Bloomfield and Tariffville. The inspired passengers sang gospel songs on the way. Six excited teenagers from the First Congregational Church in New Hartford stood on the train's platform with their mother, who urged them to keep together in the darkness.

A little after 10 P.M., with engineer George P. Hatch, forty-two years old, at the controls, the first engine, the Salisbury, pulled out of Tariffville and slowly eased onto the twin spans of the truss bridge over the Farmington River. This bridge was like most American railroad structures of the period, with wooden timbers and iron suspension rods, only 10 feet above the water. Hatch passed through the first span, but as he neared the end of the second, something happened.

Unexpectedly, the bridge collapsed, throwing the engine and its crew onto the riverbank. At the controls of the second engine, Tariffville, engineer Thomas Franey felt it lurch, roll, and crash down, taking the baggage car and three passenger cars with it. The sounds of cracking timbers and the cries of the injured filled the frigid air. Hatch, the engineer of the Salisbury, was badly scalded and died the next evening.

The conductor, T. M. Elmore, was about to enter the baggage car when he felt the rear end settling. In the corner was the stove with a very hot fire.

> My first thought was to get away from the fire so as not to be burned. There were three other men in the car, all passengers. It was very dark so that I could see nothing except the streak of light which came through the hole in the roof. Meanwhile the water was coming into the car . . . and rapidly rising. It got up . . . above our waists and stopped, when we knew that the car had struck bottom, and then we felt safer. We went to work to rescue ourselves . . . by lifting one man up to the roof and after he got through he assisted another, and then the others were helped out.

This stereograph image captures the railroad wreck on Tariffville Bridge. Imagine the terror of the thirteen passengers who were killed and the seventy who were injured. CONNECTICUT HISTORICAL SOCIETY MUSEUM

After heaving himself out of the baggage car, Jonathan Jones, the Western's superintendent, returned to the Tariffville depot and telegraphed the company's office in West Winsted: "Send extra train with surgeons and Mr. Greer [the roadmaster]. Three cars through bridge at Tariffville." Within an hour an emergency train with doctors, medical supplies, and workers was on its way. Next, Jones telegraphed the Hartford office of the Hartford, Providence & Fishkill Railroad asking for additional help. By 1 A.M. a Fishkill train was on its way with twenty more doctors. Dr. D. P. Pelletier was the first surgeon notified; he rushed to a drug store and telephoned other doctors, making what the *Courant* would claim was the world's first emergency phone call.

Meanwhile, Caleb Camp, president of the Connecticut Western, who happened to be a passenger in one of the unwrecked coaches, sought help from the village residents. Church bells summoned volunteer rescuers and spectators to the scene. Then began the grisly task of extricating the dead and wounded. The Reverend Goodnough of Winsted found himself under the water and struggled to gain a foothold on the ice; once out, he plunged into the wreck and with his strong arms began saving others. The Reverend Thomas of Winsted, despite two broken limbs, made his way out through the roof. E. R. Carter of New Hartford worked all night to search for victims. Samuel R. Johnson of South Norfolk in car number 9, which lay up and down in the river under car number 11, spent a half hour making sure the last man, George Dudley Sr., got out. Just after midnight the West Winsted special arrived, and half an hour later the Fishkill train. The latter returned to Hartford with many of the dead and some survivors, while also towing the unwrecked cars.

The rescue search resumed early Wednesday morning. A large crowd gathered upon the west bank to watch. The air was piercing cold, and fires had been kindled from pieces of the wreck. Piled upon the ground was a mass of clothing, satchels, boots, and shoes. Recovering the bodies was difficult because they were tangled among the bridge timbers and platforms and submerged under the ice-cold water. The bodies of five of the six New Hartford teenagers, who had been carried under the ice and drowned, were carried across the river on sledges.

The sixth survived. Wallace Warner of Canton found the body of his brother Howard, the ticket agent at Canton. Both had been on the train. That same day the Reverend Moody conducted a prayer service attended by 2,000 people.

Connecticut Western President Caleb Camp wrote the *Courant:*

> ... I wish to thank the passengers who were on the ill-fated train . . . for the great coolness, courage, heroism, self-sacrificing devotion, and sympathy manifested on that ever-to-be-remembered night. . . . That so few were lost in view of the fearful wreck, which is spoken of by railroad men of long experience as the most fearful they had ever witnessed, is wonderful. That there were not more than 100 lives lost seems almost a miracle.

Later that month, a jury of inquest impaneled in Simsbury to determine the cause heard more than fifty witnesses. The bridge experts believed the engine must have been derailed; J. F. Jones, the company's superintendent, concurred. But this was contradicted by a witness riding the forward engine, who said it wasn't derailed. Other railroad officials thought the bridge was weak and broke under the weight. But it was not unusual to run two engines over a wooden bridge. The jury's final verdict was split: Dome felt the bridge was sound, but the tender of the Salisbury may have derailed and struck exposed trusses. Others said that the bitter cold weather had weakened the bridge and the huge weight of the special train had brought it down.

In all thirteen died and seventy were injured. Connecticut Western paid $200 to $600 for each life lost. The engines were raised, repaired, and returned to service. The bridge was rebuilt on the same design. Even before the accident, the railroad's financial condition had been weak, and now it could not pay off its mounting debts. On April 28, 1880, the railroad's mortgage was foreclosed, and the company went bankrupt.

There was another significant train disaster before the end of the century—a spectacular affair involving the collision of four trains but, strangely enough, with only two fatalities, both crewmen. December 4, 1891, dawned foggy in the hamlet of East Thompson, in the northeast corner of the state, 10 miles east of Putnam, a nerve center for the New York & New England Railroad. At Putnam the twin track Eastern Division crossed the company's Norwich & Worcester Division. On this morning three of the four trains soon to be involved were in the vicinity of Putnam: the fast-approaching eastbound Long Island and Eastern States express, a ready-to-leave Boston-bound freight express, and the Norwich steamboat express, which would be switched over to track 2 at Putnam for the fast run to Boston. The fourth train, the Southbridge local freight in East Thompson, was getting ready.

Thus, the Boston train dispatcher had three trains to handle at once without delaying their schedules. Eastern States would take track 2. The slower freight number 212 to Boston he put on the westbound track number 1 to run east. The bold, unorthodox move was necessary to get both trains out of Putnam and clear the way for the Norwich express. Unfortunately, the dispatcher forgot about the local freight. Engineer Joe Page, hearing a shrill whistle in the distance and then seeing the yellowish glow of a headlight at the train rounded the curve of the same track as his, yelled to his fireman, "Head for the woods!" Both then jumped from the cab. Number 212 plowed into the local freight with a loud crash. Ruptured steam shot heavenward.

Now, the Eastern States, unaware of the wreckage ahead, rounded the same curve minutes later and crashed into the debris spewed on track 2. Its engine derailed, doing a 180-degree turn and burying itself in sand and gravel, killing engineer Harry Taber and fireman Gerry Fitzgerald. The badly shaken passengers in two Pullman sleepers stumbled outside in the cold dawn. The time was 6:47. But what about the Norwich steamboat express? A flagman was sent out—too late. The boat train rammed into the rear of the Eastern States. Miraculously, no one was seriously hurt. One of the seventy-five passengers, an Irishman, fresh from the home country, clutched cages of goldfinches and asked, "Is this Boston?"

LET IT SNOW, LET IT SNOW, LET IT SNOW

The Great Blizzard
1888

New Englanders talk more about the weather than any other subject. In casual conversation the usual greeting is, first, "How are you," and then quickly, "What's it going to do today?" That's because changes occur so often and unpredictably. Hartford's Samuel Clemens (aka Mark Twain) said it best:

> There is a sumptuous variety about the New England weather that compels the stranger's admiration—and regret. . . . The weather is always doing something there. In the Spring I have counted 136 different kinds of weather inside of 24 hours: probable nor'east to sou'west winds, varying to the southard and westard and points between; high and low barometer, sweeping around from place to place; probable areas of rain, snow, hail, and drought, succeeded or preceded by earthquakes with thunder and lightning.

Actually, New England is less vulnerable to natural calamities like blizzards and hurricanes than other areas. Historically, the average number of pleasant days per year is almost 200.

*Horses carried away loads of snow in the cleanup from the
"Great Blizzard of 1888."* CONNECTICUT HISTORICAL SOCIETY MUSEUM

But severe storms leave a lasting impression, not only in the meteorological records but also in the folklore of the region, beginning with the chronicler Cotton Mather in Massachusetts Bay in 1635. Connecticut is seldom trashed by tornados, although in August 1878 one struck Wallingford over a 2-mile area and killed thirty-four persons. All but one were Irish immigrants. Ice storms are more frequent and can wreak greater damage than blizzards. On December 16, 1973, a northeaster coated trees and utility lines with ice more than an inch thick that cut off power for several days.

No storm, however, seems to have been more intense or better remembered than the Great Blizzard of 1888. In early March a massive northeaster settled over Block Island and pummeled southern New England with gale force winds, near zero temperatures, and up to 50 inches of snow.

When Elizabeth Jarvis Colt, the grande dame of Hartford society and the widow of the gun maker Samuel Colt, went to bed in her palatial Armsmear home in Hartford on Sunday, March 11, the weather was mild for that time of year—in fact the mildest winter in seventeen years, around forty degrees and raining. At 2 A.M., awakened by a rattling of the window panes, she looked out to see blinding sheets of snow pushed about by a fury of wind. In the morning the city was being buried under 3 feet of wet snow. As far as she could see up Wethersfield Avenue toward Main Street, there lay enormous drifts, some 10 to 12 feet high. Nothing moved. There was an eerie silence. New England's worst storm since the advent of the railroad and telegraph had paralyzed the city.

All day the storm continued to blow hard. Snow stopped falling about Tuesday noon, though the wind howled until dark. Mrs. Colt wondered how the Colt Armory was doing. She was informed by her coachman that like most of the other factories in Hartford, the Armory had been closed. Unable to get home, many workers had spent the night near their machines or sought shelter with strangers. Eight young women stranded outside the plant were rescued when, like Alpine climbers, they were roped together and pulled by men at the head of the line, who broke a path through the snow for them. Downtown, businessmen gave up any thought of getting home that night, even if it was only a short journey, and instead crowded into hotels. On North Main Street boys raided cans of frozen milk, left on abandoned milk sleighs, and had ice cream for supper. The *Courant* reported: "A trip of a few hundred yards in the teeth of the storm tried the nerve and muscle of the strongest and was often attended with personal peril." But the *Courant*'s enterprising newsboys reaped a bonanza. Instead of the usual two cents a copy they earned up to fifty cents.

A hearse bearing the remains of James Mullaly overturned; the undertakers found an express wagon to carry him into the Blue Hills Cemetery, where he was safely interred. Mrs. Charles Sealim was aroused by a loud cracking noise; she awakened her husband, who kept a livery stable, and along with two snowbound milkmen passing the night with them, they escaped from the house just as the roof and walls caved in. Their eleven horses were unharmed. Caspar Kreutzer, after an enjoyable outing at Koch's saloon, became so confused as to his whereabouts that he ended up in a deep snowbank. Two alert young men retrieved him. The train from Boston was blocked by a snowdrift when it reached Vernon, and fifty-two passengers were marooned in the local depot until Wednesday night.

Fortunately, Wednesday dawned clear and mild. The good weather brought people outdoors to marvel at the drifts, and as they are wont to do in an emergency, they good-naturedly lent a hand where needed. Not a sidewalk or street was passable. Youngsters overcame this difficulty creatively by making snowshoes out of boards or barrel staves. Eight-horse teams with plows were put to work clearing the tracks of the horse railway. When the Pratt & Whitney factory on Capitol Avenue exhausted its coal supply that afternoon, a procession of several employees, joined by others from the nearby shops of Weed Sewing Machine and Hartford Machine Screw, marched down to the Commerce Street coal yard, attached ropes to a sleigh laden with two tons of coal, and dragged the fuel back to the plant.

Good humor prevailed. In front of the Allyn House barber shop, atop an immense snow tunnel, was a sign, THIS WAY TO

Business came to a standstill on Temple Street, where snow blocked
the entrances to Jacobs & Proctors Opera House, a dental office,
and an art supply store in post-blizzard Hartford.
CONNECTICUT HISTORICAL SOCIETY MUSEUM

THE CHINESE LAUNDRY. Another sign, pointing north along the
solid white mass that hid Main Street, read: THIS WAY TO TEM-
PLE STREET. KEEP OFF THE GRASS. Outside the Opera House a pair
of men's shoes, soles up, stuck out of a large drift; some wag
had placed a board behind them with the inscription: REMAINS
OF STEVE CLARK.

Except for paths made by the footprints of shoppers armed
with baskets on their way to the grocery stores, most streets
were still blocked on Thursday. The Horse Railway Company
had 300 men clearing tracks. Mrs. Colt was pleased to observe
a blue car pulled by four horses on a return trip from Asylum
Street. Another team was dispatched to escort the president of
the Jewell Belt factory to his home on Washington Street from

an enforced stay at the Allyn House. The Union for Home Work, which Mrs. Colt had founded, could hardly keep up with the calls for relief. Mayor Morgan Bulkeley paid a visit to its director and encouraged her to provide the needy with coal and food and to send him the bills. On Friday the Belle of Hartford omnibus sleigh made it from downtown west to the city line, where in the vicinity of Mark Twain's house on Forest Street, residents were finding the easiest way to exit their homes was by means of ladders from their second-story windows. By Saturday transportation within and from the city was running again, and, miraculously, business was back to normal. In his sermon on Sunday, the mathematical minister of Center Congregational Church computed the volume of snow dumped on Connecticut: 15,457 billion cubic feet by his calculation!

Elsewhere in the state the storm created similar disruptions, especially to the transportation and telegraph systems. Connecticut's extensive railroad network was vital to moving goods and people. Now, trains from New Haven or Boston were blocked by drifts. Superintendent Davidson of the Consolidated Railroad said, "I never saw anything like this in my thirty-one years' experience on this road. It could not be better expressed than by saying we are paralyzed." The *Hartford Courant* reported that on "Tuesday morning the state was nearly as devoid of means of communication as it was a century ago." The express from Boston to Springfield spent forty hours in a snowdrift at Indian Orchard near Wilbraham, Massachusetts. Local townspeople broke paths to it, bringing provisions to the dining car and fuel for the engine. The passengers whiled away the hours of their imprisonment by singing and listening to lectures by a former consul to Jerusalem and a missionary to China. Two actresses performed. An unexpected climax was the birth of a baby, the actresses rallying to the emergency as if they were trained nurses.

Another westbound train on the New England Railroad, which left Boston on Monday, ran on time as far as Vernon, where it encountered an immovable drift. The fifty-three passengers partied despite their dismal surroundings, christening the depot the "Vernon Hotel." One genius devised a "Bill of Air," a specimen of choreography, and set forth such dishes as "Alligators stuffed with clam shells" and "Crabs picked off with boxing gloves." The train was finally dug out and reached Hartford at 11 P.M. Wednesday. That same morning, an attempt had been made to force a way from Hartford on both the Consolidated and Valley lines. One, made up of two engines and one car of shovelers, got through to Springfield. The other was stalled below Middletown. By Friday the tracks were cleared from Boston to Hartford, but not from New York north.

New Haven called the storm the most terrible ever known, the streets impossible for teams and drifts piled from 10 to 40 feet high. The New York & New Haven Railroad had a dozen engines disabled or off the track, as well as thirty freight and passenger trains stalled on various divisions. For two days Wethersfield used large gangs of men, horses, and oxen to force passages through its main streets. New London reported the rescue of two little boys, ages nine and four, who had been buried under 3 feet of snow for an entire day. They had been left alone at home when they decided to venture out across three lots to rejoin their mother, who was visiting a sick relative. Soon exhausted, they crawled behind a stone wall and were covered by snow. A search party, including their father, finally discovered a cap and mitten on a path leading to the wall. Digging down, they found the children barely alive. Back home, their frostbitten hands and ears were wrapped in cloths saturated with molasses. They recovered.

Altogether, New England suffered 400 deaths and $20 million in property damage from the Great Blizzard. It moved the *Courant* to reflect editorially:

> Such a storm as this, had it come 100 years ago, would not have caused a fiftieth part of the inconvenience. It is the boasting and progressive Nineteenth Century that is paralyzed, while the slow going Eighteenth Century would have taken such an experience without a ruffle. . . . It is our "advantages" that have gone back on us. . . . There is no railroad any longer, no telegraph, no horse car, no milk, no delivery of food at the door. We starve in the midst of plenty.

What would the same editor have written if he had lived fifty years later during the flood of 1936 or the hurricane of 1938 when we had the additional conveniences of automobiles, telephones, and radios?

C H A P T E R 1 2

THINGS THAT GO BANG! IN THE NIGHT

The Park Central Explosion

1889

In the late 1880s the population of Hartford grew to over 50,000. It was a bustling, booming metropolis of insurance companies and factories. The number of immigrants had peaked, led by the Irish and Germans. There were 222 licensed saloons and numerous prostitutes. The streets were lighted by electricity. The new state capitol over Bushnell Park dominated the skyline. Below on Trinity Street was the newly dedicated brownstone arch of the Soldiers and Sailors Memorial. The blue onion-shaped dome of the great Colt Armory was another well-known landmark. Samuel Colt's widow, Elizabeth Jarvis Colt, was still society's grande dame. It was nothing for her to entertain 200 for lunch, dinner, or a lawn fete. The Great Blizzard of Monday, March 12, 1888, during which 30 inches of snow had fallen in four days and temporarily paralyzed the city, was still a topic of conversation. Another important event of the time was the introduction of Colonel Pope's safety bicycle, launching the bicycle craze in America

and making Pope Manufacturing the country's leading manufacturer.

Downtown, on Allyn Street, stood the rather decrepit five-
story Park Central Hotel, which catered mainly to permanent
boarders and traveling salesmen. It was owned by Wellington
Ketchem, who lived there with his wife and their black-and-
tan dog.

In room 10 on the second floor, Lizzie Guilder, a regular
boarder, woke up thirsty at 4:30 A.M. on Sunday, February 17,
1889. Opening her door, she saw George Gaines, the black
porter, passing along the hall and asked him to bring her a
pitcher of ice water. After what seemed a long wait, she stepped
into the hall and through the speaking tube called down to
Edward Perry, the night clerk. Just as she turned away, Lizzie
felt the floor rise under her feet, and with that a rush of air
pushed her toward the door of her room. At the same moment
she heard a sharp explosion followed by an earthquakelike
shock. Seizing her hat and coat, she ran back into the hall as it
collapsed under her feet and escaped by a stairway in the
annex. Downstairs behind the counter Perry was instantly
killed, while the porter met the same fate in the act of getting
Miss Guilder's water.

Soon after, the mail clerk from the Hartford depot was
running at full speed past the hotel toward the firehouse to
give the alarm. He was accosted by a man wearing a plug hat,
a balbriggan wrapper, and his underclothes. "Tell me, young
fella, where can I find the home of a clerk who works in a
clothing store?" He apparently hadn't noticed that by this
time the hotel had sunk into a mass of burning rubbish.
Except for the eastern wing, not one brick remained upon
another.

As shown in this 1889 photograph by F. L. Hale of Manchester, 300 men worked in a rescue and recovery effort after an entire city block exploded. Furnished rooms are exposed as a tower was blown in half. CONNECTICUT HISTORICAL SOCIETY MUSEUM

Daylight revealed a terrifying scene: firemen spraying hoses, bodies protruding from the debris, rescuers already probing the remains. It was a dreary morning, rainy and chilly. As is true of almost every disaster scene, the curious began to gather. By the end of the day, extra cars had to be attached to trains from Windsor and New Britain for those who yearned to see death and destruction firsthand. The governor, Morgan G. Bulkeley, called out four companies of the National Guard, who were alerted by twenty-two strokes of the fire bell, to drive back the sightseers.

Soon 300 men worked with ropes, crowbars, and bare hands. Shortly after noon, Walter Gray, a traveler for the Higganum Manufacturing Company, was rescued still lying in his bed. According to his account, he didn't hear the explosion but awoke among falling bricks. Though pinned by a heavy beam and a jumble of lath and plaster, he was unhurt and able to breathe through the thick smoke. What really worried him was that he might drown from the water being poured onto the fire and rising up to his shoulders. Shivering from head to foot, he declared himself ready to go to work if only he could get some clothes.

After being buried for eight hours, the hotel proprietor, his wife, and dog were also brought out safely. Another couple, Mr. and Mrs. Maximilian Galody, were not so lucky. The publisher of the *Hartford Herald*, Galody was a recent German immigrant. Ten persons were still alive, but twenty-two bodies, some charred beyond recognition, were uncovered by rescuers working until 2 A.M.

One of the casualties was William Seymour, the stationary engineer on duty. The investigation proved he was also the cause of the explosion: He had forgotten to maintain the water level in the boiler.

WORSE THAN WORLD WAR I

The Influenza Epidemic
1918–1919

Called the Spanish Influenza, it was one of the world's three most destructive human epidemics, claiming over twenty-one million lives in 1918–1919, about twice the number killed in World War I. From September to December in 1918, it caused an estimated 500,000 deaths in the United States, five times as many as the number of American soldiers who died in France. No treatment was found to be of value, and of course there were then no antibiotics or flu vaccines. One day a victim might feel nauseated and go to bed with a headache; the next day, he or she might be dead.

In the summer of 1918, New London was a busy transit port for soldiers and sailors returning from Europe as the war neared its end. By the middle of July, the German chancellor knew that all was lost. General Pershing said the counterattack at Soissons had turned the tide of the war. Next, the Meuse-Argonne offensive of September 26, which involved the greatest number of American troops who had ever fought, was the final blow, though an armistice was not signed until November 11.

The transports disembarked thousands, including the wounded and sick. Among the patients were some who carried a deadly virus. On September 1, several cases of flu that originated at the Experimental Station at Fort Trumbull were reported by the naval hospital. Within a day or two, more cases came from the submarine base located 2 miles above New London. By September 10, a hundred cases filled the hospital. The sickness continued to spread like wildfire: to the government station on the State Pier, where 300 men from the Boston Navy Yard had just arrived; to civilian homes, where nearly 7,000 sailors were billeted. Other cases appeared throughout the state among soldiers on leave from Camp Devens in Ayer, Massachusetts. By the end of the month, the total number of cases reported was 901, and a month later there were 936 more.

The disease began suddenly with chilliness, fever, and pain in the legs, head, and eyes. Backaches were often severe. When ears, lips, and face became ashen, death soon followed. The final stage was a purple color in the face, a sign of cyanosis from lack of oxygen. Body temperatures were in the 103- to 104-degree range. Not all cases were fatal: in one study of 1,668 cases among almost 6,000 troops, only 19 percent of those infected died. The disease affected younger persons the most often; after age thirty-five only 20 percent of the population became ill, and over age fifty-one only 10 percent.

Besides the New London port situation, several factors contributed to the state's special vulnerability. One was the crowded conditions of troop ships and military camps. Another was the congestion in industrialized urban areas, filled with recent European emigrants susceptible to airborne contagion and working in poorly ventilated factories. The infection spread from east to west—to Willimantic, Hartford, New Britain, Meriden, and Waterbury, and south to New Haven and Bridgeport. In Waterbury, of the 1,701 deaths from September 1918 through March 1919, 63 percent were from influenza.

Those without access to hospitals or medical advice relied on old folk remedies to get well. The sick were sent to bed and covered with warm blankets. They sprinkled sulphur in their shoes, wore vinegar packs on their stomachs, tied slices of cucumber to each ankle, or carried a potato in each pocket. Doctors who did make house calls prescribed pills that were powerless to help. Most of those stricken, however, recovered.

During the epidemic 101 nurses and 48 physicians from outside the state were sent to the neediest communities. Thirty-five emergency hospitals were either set up, supervised, or assisted by the state's Department of Health. Hartford Hospital was so overwhelmed with patients that it closed its surgical wards. Joseph Camp, eight years old at the time, spent three weeks there. According to the *Courant,* he kept asking the nurses every day, "How's Ma?" And every day he got the same answer: "Fine." At age eighty-three he remembered the

> warm blankets, hot blankets. I was screaming, "Nurse, nurse, I'm sweating." She says, "You're supposed to sweat." I remember coming home and the first thing I'm saying is, "Where's Ma? Where's Ma?" And finally my sister told me. She was gone.

His mother, Genevieve, an Italian immigrant, had died.

The city asked the hospital to use the Hartford Golf Club for patients; it was opened on October 17, and the city's churches urged its members to volunteer to help. The schools in West Hartford and Willimantic were closed. Charles Begley recalled waiting on a chilly November Monday outside St. Joseph's School in Hartford: "The head sister came to the window and said, 'Sorry, you have to go home. The sisters are sick.'" The school reopened three weeks later.

Though the Health Department did not ban public gatherings, in theaters the following message was flashed on the screens: "The health authorities will close this theater unless spitting, coughing or sneezing is omitted during performances. Sneezing and coughing . . . may spread influenza. Be fair and stay home if you have a cold."

Pity the poor soul who couldn't help a sneeze or cough. The show would stop and another slide would be projected: "The person sneezing or coughing will please retire now in the interest of the health of those sitting near him."

From September 1918 through May 1919, 115,720 Connecticut residents got the flu. It killed almost 9,000 people in the state—nearly 1 percent of the state's 1.2 million population. The worst month was October, when 5,228 persons died. In 1918 Windham County had the highest morbidity rate; in 1919, as the epidemic moved westward, it was Litchfield County. During the same period pneumonia claimed 2,336 lives, making a total of over 11,000 deaths statewide.

In April 1919 the Connecticut Health Bulletin reminded the public that "the epidemic of influenza was a blasting thing, many times more devastating than the war. It was proportionately as harmful to the population of Connecticut as was any year of the war to any of the belligerents engaged." Aside from the tragedy the amazing thing is the lack of attention it received from the press, which was focused on the military and diplomatic developments abroad. Military histories do not mention it. Influenza was not then a commonly reportable disease. In the atmosphere of 1918 the epidemic was possibly regarded by the patriotic public as an incident in the war—another battle fought on the home front.

Some researchers since then claim that flu was not the killer: It weakened the body to become a host to deadly bacterial infection, mainly pneumonia. In 1976 the nation panicked when a soldier at Fort Dix died of swine flu. President Gerald R. Ford initiated the most massive immunization in history, with forty-five million doses given. Today, despite the widespread use of annual flu vaccines, thousands still die of flu each year.

EVEN COLT GOT SOAKED

The Great Flood
1936

Nothing as devastating had occurred before in the Connecticut Valley. In March and April every year, people were accustomed to heavy rain, melting snow, and rising rivers and streams. But 1936 was different. On March 11, a warm rain poured down on the snow-laden valley. Far upstream in Vermont and New Hampshire, the heavy snow blanket began to melt rapidly into the tributaries of the Connecticut River. As the swollen streams churned into the river itself, the flood gauge rose 6 inches every hour.

Near Windsor, where the Farmington and Connecticut Rivers join, a tremendous ice jam had formed, 20 feet high and 3 miles long. At about 3 P.M. Friday, it broke up and with an ominous rumble moved downstream toward Hartford. Although the water level climbed to 24 feet, the flood seemed to have reached its crest on Sunday; it actually receded a few feet during the next two days. But more torrential rain and unseasonably warm weather followed. By midnight, Wednesday, March 18, the river had risen to 25 feet. Meteorologists would call it a 500-year or even a 1,000-year flood.

The worst was yet to come. Before dawn the next day, the tossing and turbulent river had leapt 5 feet, higher than ever before. The old record had supposedly been set in 1927, but it was not as memorable an event in Hartford history as the rain-caused flood of May 1, 1854. Then water rose over 30 feet in front of Colt's Armory and tested the strength of the unfinished dike that Col. Samuel Colt, at his own expense and despite the ridicule of the Hartford Court of Common Council, was building around his property. Extending nearly 2 miles, this earthen embankment with willows planted on top ranged from 40 to 100 feet wide and reached as high as 32 feet. The dike held and saved the new armory then under construction.

During that flood laborers who lived in shanties in the South Meadows had to be removed by boat. Unable to sail because the coal yards were underwater, the steamer *City of Hartford* used lifeboats to rescue stranded families. The rest of the city looked like an island.

Pleased with his foresight, Colt boldly announced that "if the city will relieve my property from taxation, I will bind myself to exclude the river from the South Meadows; and, more than all that, if the city will pay for it, I will agree to dike the Connecticut River from end to end so that nothing less than Noah's flood can reach the houses which are now inundated."

The council spurned his offer but did extend the dike upriver toward the covered bridge, and in 1929 spent $1 million for another extension south to Wethersfield.

For eighty years the Colt dike had protected the Armory and its environs. Now, on Friday, it appeared that Noah's flood indeed threatened the city. Water was flowing at the rate of 300,000 cubic feet a second—sixty times faster than normal.

During the Great Flood of 1938, the author of this book left Harvard for a weekend home in Connecticut. When his train arrived in Hartford, he discovered Union Station had become an island. Looking up Asylum Street, he saw a rowboat emerge from the Hotel Bond, the building on the right side of this photo.
CONNECTICUT HISTORICAL SOCIETY MUSEUM

The bridge to East Hartford was closed at noon. In the meadows the electric light plant was cut off from land; the crew inside did its best to hold back the water from the boilers. At the same time hundreds of people were being evacuated from the East Side as the streets in that low area became a new bottom for the river. Rats scurried for dry land.

Three hundred American Legion volunteers, assisted by Boy Scouts, Work Progress Administration workers, and the Governor's Foot Guard, rowed or paddled boats through the swirling eddies of canals newly formed around the tenements. Young and old, clutching bundles and suitcases, waited on second-floor verandas to be rescued. Some irrepressible souls, however, turned the calamity into a frolic. Like Venetian gondoliers, some Italians in canoes floated down Front Street carrying jugs of wine and playing mandolins.

Seeing a chance to make a quick profit, a few rascals launched homemade craft and ferried anyone willing to pay $2.00, until the police put a stop to the racket. Policemen also patrolled the area in outboards to prevent looting. The arrival of Coast Guard whaleboats sped up the evacuation process. After touring the downtown district, Mayor Thomas Spellacy announced that his office would be open around the clock for the rest of the emergency.

At Red Cross headquarters wild confusion reigned as frenzied people sought help in locating relatives or having them removed to safety. In the meantime the water slowly spread westward, up the Park River toward the hotels, office buildings, banks, and insurance companies near Bushnell Park.

It soaked the generators of the transit company's powerhouse in the South Meadows, and all trolley cars stalled on their tracks. At St. Anthony's Church on Talcott Street, water sloshed down one side of the nave, while on the other huddled worshipers celebrated Mass. Later, a body was found floating in the vestibule. Fear-maddened animals in the zoo at Colt Park were shot as an act of mercy.

Thursday night found the center of the city in darkness and the river 4 feet higher. Candle vendors appeared, hawking three puny tapers, worth a nickel, for twenty-five cents. All day, city engineers and a crew of hundreds had labored to raise the Colt dike with sandbags. Around 11 P.M., however, the raging, muddy water surged over the top, raced along the meadows toward the Armory, tore the huge tanks of an oil depot from their foundations, and threatened the power station. Within minutes the entire first floor and 2 feet of the second floor of the Colt factory were under water. Quarter-ton molds were upended and sheets of steel thrown around like tissue paper.

Three hours later, a 20-foot wall of water roared through Hartford's squatter village south of the Armory, smashing the shacks into pieces. The screaming inhabitants found themselves instantly engulfed by water and debris. In the dark they battered down doors, pried up roofs, and struggled to escape. As they waded in every direction, the demolished dwellings swirled past them, knocking them down again and again. Luckily, rescue craft were nearby to haul them away from the water.

The third day, Friday, was the longest. All the utilities except gas were crippled. As much as 50,000 tons of coal had been swept downstream. A gloom descended on the city. Telephones were out of order, the radio stations operated by battery; National Guardsmen as well as policemen patrolled the streets.

At 8 A.M. Saturday the river crested at 37.56 feet—6 feet above the previous record and the highest the river has ever gone. One-fifth of the city was inundated. Almost 10,000 refugees crowded schools and other relief centers or were cared for by relatives and friends.

Fearful of looting and vandalism by those who had no business in the city, police and military officials barred all sightseeing automobiles from downtown, issued passes to those engaged in relief work, and declared a midnight curfew. Relief workers and refugees received the first of the 25,000 typhoid shots that were administered.

By Sunday night the river had retreated 2 feet, and electric service had been restored. Mayor Spellacy met with his department heads to plan a massive cleanup program. The rain

This aerial photo shows Hartford largely submerged during the 1938 flood.
CONNECTICUT HISTORICAL SOCIETY MUSEUM

stopped and the cold March winds took over. The curfew remained in effect.

Early Monday morning, 8,000 workers began the dismal process of bringing the flood zone back to life. A flying squad inspected the shoreline and found most of the structures safe for reoccupancy. The Board of Aldermen voted an emergency appropriation of $500,000 for relief and rehabilitation. The Fire Department worried about the thousands of gallons of gasoline that had leaked into the river from the dislodged oil tanks. People were cautioned about fallen live wires on the streets and waterlogged insulation inside the buildings. Armed with shovels, axes, and mops, men from out-of-town Civilian Conservation Corps camps dug out cellars and disinfected homes with chlorinated lime.

The mud was knee deep, oil coated the sides of buildings, and everything standing dripped and stank. Underneath, the pavement had been peeled back in hundreds of places and curbstones stood almost on end. One man stepped into one of the deep pits and immediately drowned. The Italian and Jewish shopkeepers returning to their East Side stores were greeted by a jumbled mass of soaked, battered, and buried litter. Cleanup crews shoveled the mess from shop to curb, where it formed a 6-foot-high mound. These small merchants faced ruin.

At Colt's the water level was marked at 38.6 feet, 6 feet above the demolished dike. No one could get inside the building until Sunday, March 22. Twenty feet of water still surrounded the plant. To fill a rush order for 200 automatic pistols, shipping clerks carried the boxes to the window sills on the second story and loaded them on motorboats from there.

James Kinnarney, who lived nearby on Huyshope Avenue, had never seen anything like it in his nearly fifty years of working at Colt's. The inside of his house and all his furniture ruined, Kinnarney set out to salvage what he could from his office. The only way he could reach it was to commandeer a skiff with an outboard, and with a couple of helpers he chugged along the second floor, skirting in and out of the machinery. He managed to retrieve a few papers. A quick survey revealed that every machine would have to be dismantled and cleaned and every motor dried or rewound. Tons of silt covered the machinery and walls of the ground floor; the aisles were sand dunes 2 feet high.

The devastation tested the leadership of Connecticut's seventy-six-year-old governor, Wilbur "Toby" Cross, a Yale professor of English literature. During his eight-year tenure, he'd earned the affection of most citizens for his Yankee sense of humor and thrift, he made the governorship a full-time job, and he led the state's recovery from its two worst natural disasters: the flood of 1936 and the hurricane of 1938.

Touring the area, Cross said the hardest hit was near the Colt dike. The bleak houses behind the Armory were submerged or abandoned, except for wandering cats. Colt Park had become a lake; through the shattered lead glass of the Church of the Good Shepard one could see prayer books and hymnals floating. Men in boats, returning distressed owners to their homes or possessions, plied back and forth. Along the railroad spur between the Armory and the river, freight cars lay on their sides, the tracks twisted and torn. Yawning holes marked what had been sidewalks. Refuse hung from poles and wires. A crude doll sat forlornly on top of a wire fence. Chugging steam pumps sucked water back into the Park River. And from the fetid water rose a stench that no one quite forgot.

In the thirty-five-town area, covering the 100 square miles flooded by the Connecticut River, the total physical damage was estimated at $35 million, of which two-thirds was in Hartford alone. Amazingly enough, only five persons lost their lives.

As a result of the 1936 flood and a hurricane two years later, the dike was strengthened and elevated to 45 feet, and Hartford's separation from its historic riverfront began, not to be reclaimed until the launching of Riverfront Recapture in the 1980s.

THE BIGGEST BLOW OF THEM ALL

The Great Hurricane
1938

In the borough of Fenwick, Old Saybrook, at the mouth of the Connecticut River, most of the summer residents had left after Labor Day. But the Hepburn family stayed on in their shingled home facing Long Island Sound. September 21 dawned bright. Katharine was elated that her new play, *The Philadelphia Story,* was headed for Broadway. She took her usual morning swim and played a round of golf on the Fenwick nine-hole course. The wind began to rise, and on the par-three ninth, her ball flew straight for the hole. Her first hole in one and a record 31 for the nine holes!

As the storm gathered strength that morning, Mrs. Thomas N. Hepburn was reading the latest play of George Bernard Shaw. Shaw was her favorite author, and nothing could disturb her concentration. But her daughter; her son Dick, an aspiring playwright; Jack Hammond, Dick's college friend; and their old nurse Fanny were increasingly alarmed as the water rose, windows blew in, and the wind howled louder than ever before. They were used to severe storms from the southwest, but this morning was different.

Mrs. Hepburn pooh-poohed their concerns. "Call Stanley," she said, "and have him come and board up the windows." As soon as the carpenter arrived, his Model A Ford blew over into the lagoon on the north side of the house. A shell-shock casualty of World War I, he was in no condition to repair windows. By then the water had risen to the windowsills; Dick finally convinced his mother this was no ordinary storm and led them out through a window. He had to carry Fanny, who weighed a solid 200 pounds. As they reached higher ground, they looked back. The house suddenly disintegrated. In her autobiography *Me* Katharine recalled:

> It just sailed away—easy as pie—and soon there was nothing at all left on the spot where the house had stood for over sixty years. Our house—ours for 25 years—all our possessions—just gone.

All gone except for the third floor, which serenely floated east toward the Connecticut River. The next morning, they found the floor intact with Dick's typewriter and latest manuscript still reposing on the desk.

After Labor Day some of the summer residents had left behind a few servants to close up their homes for the winter. Katharine gathered up the frightened domestics and took them to the closed Riversea Inn for the night. Candles provided the only light. Just as she settled down, she had the good sense to see that every candle had been extinguished. Sure enough, in the hall she found one about to topple over that might have set the whole place on fire. The next few days, she spent digging among the ruins of the Hepburn cottage, recovering some of the family silver. Without delay she and her father, Dr. Hepburn,

Katharine Hepburn surveys the destruction of the 1938 hurricane at her family's summer cottage in Fenwick. CONNECTICUT HISTORICAL SOCIETY MUSEUM

decided to build a much larger brick home on the same spot. He was heard to exclaim: "I'll not let old Neptune get the better of me!"

September 21, 1938, was a day always to be remembered in Connecticut. There was no warning of the storm to come, and nothing like it had happened in 123 years. It started in Africa's Sahara Desert and moved westward into the Atlantic over the Cape Verde Islands. By the evening of September 16, weather experts in America recognized it as a full-fledged hurricane but felt it would miss the mainland. Then, it began to curve to the north between two high-pressure areas from the east, leaving a narrow corridor of warm, moist air pointed at New England. Suddenly, on September 21, it accelerated. By 11 A.M. the center lay east of Norfolk, Virginia; two hours later, it was off New Jersey, racing at 70 miles per hour toward Long Island, and as it crossed the Long Island Sound, it was traveling at up to 100 miles per hour. The barometric pressure fell to 27.94 inches, the lowest ever recorded on land in the Northeast.

Among the first to feel the impact were the thirty passengers and crew on the Bridgeport–Port Jefferson ferry. The old steamer, never intended to cope with anything but a Long Island squall, was struck in the middle of the Sound. Waves drowned her fires; the engines went dead. With no lights she drifted helplessly. After a night of terror, she was towed safely into Bridgeport Harbor by the Coast Guard.

After four days of heavy rains, the weather was very warm and muggy, and at 2 P.M. on the fifth day, the rain fell again in torrents. Soon, a gigantic wall of black-green salt water smashed against the shores of Connecticut, Rhode Island, and Massachusetts. The ocean tides, already at their fullest flood

The Connecticut shoreline was devastated by the 1938 hurricane, as shown in this photo taken in Madison. CONNECTICUT HISTORICAL SOCIETY MUSEUM

because of the autumnal equinox, rose 10 to 17 feet above normal. Nine bodies washed ashore at Westbrook.

Along the shoreline the crack New Haven passenger train, the Bostonian, passing over the narrow Stonington causeway, grinded to a halt as the tower man flashed a red danger signal. Engineer Harry Easton climbed down from his engine and walked to the tower to get permission to cross. Water was licking the tracks. Before he got to the engine, the water was up to his hips. The car windows began to go on the seaward side. Beneath the tracks, unseen, the rail bed was disappearing. The 175 passengers were ordered to move up to the front cars. Easton saw people leaping in terror from the windows, doors, and platforms into the water. Elvine Richard, seventeen years old, and her mother were dragged down by the undertow; a tree branch broke Elvine's leg, but two students pulled her out. Ed Flanagan from Providence remembered that

> boats and houses were hurled up against the side of the train. . . . Passengers clung to the cables and engine wheels. Some of them were finally swept away.

The train was now on an island, and Easton saw that unless he could uncouple the front cars, what remained of the Bostonian was doomed. The rear cars had jackknifed and lay on their sides. This heroic feat was accomplished by the brakeman, Bill Donoghue. Blowing his whistle, Easton opened the throttle all the way. The engine began to move slowly, while women and children "clustered like flies" on its sides. The engineer described the final push to the Stonington station for *Railroad* magazine:

> Crates, logs and small boats kept smashing our locomotive. . . . A full-sized sailboat, tilted on one side, was lodged on the track. . . . My hand could feel the deep vibration as the engine's power drove against the heavy barrier of wood. We were stopped now, maybe for the last time. Then something snapped.

The sailboat turned bottom up and bumped its way to shore. Reaching the Stonington station, the resourceful Easton thanked God they were safe.

The New London waterfront was a chaotic mass of smashed boats of all types and sizes; sunken piers shattered

Service on the railroad was resumed two days later by using buses to carry
passengers between Old Saybrook and Westerly, Rhode Island. About 30 miles
of track had to be relaid. Full service was reestablished on October 4.
CONNECTICUT HISTORICAL SOCIETY MUSEUM

buildings, crashing trees dragged down power lines. A fire
swept through the business district, causing $4 million in
damages. Firemen, floundering in water up to their necks, the
gale blowing the stream from their hoses back in their faces,
had a hopeless task. Every light in the city went out with the
exception of those in the Mohican Hotel, which had its own
power plant. At Ocean Beach the tidal wave lifted fifty or more
large cottages and piled them in heaps on the main road. Likewise, at other beaches from Madison to Mystic, the summer
cottages were torn asunder. Some believed the total would be
as many as 700 to 1,000. Most of the deaths caused by the
storm occurred along the shore.

In town after town, soaked and wind-blown trees toppled, adding to destruction caused by the hurricane itself. This photo was taken on Prospect Avenue in Hartford. CONNECTICUT HISTORICAL SOCIETY MUSEUM

When the storm roared inland, it toppled hundreds of trees and tore off roofs in town after town. In the harbor at Essex, one hundred high-priced yachts were wrecked or sunk; docks and floats were in shambles. Many of the majestic trees in this pretty village lay on the ground. In Deep River's Fountain Cemetery, it was estimated that 500 trees had been uprooted. In Middletown one hundred families lost their homes. The trees on the campus of Wesleyan University were gone, along with those on High Street, which the novelist Charles Dickens once had called "the most beautiful street in America." Farmers in the surrounding countryside surveyed their ruined orchards. Apples littered the ground, late summer vegetables were ruined, and livestock drowned.

In Hartford, in a repetition of the 1936 flood, the inhabitants struggled against the rapidly rising Connecticut River
after earlier rains. Without warning, they were struck from
behind at 4 P.M. by shrieking winds of 80 miles per hour, the
highest ever recorded. The clock in the Old State House
stopped at 4 P.M. Down went trees, poles, wires; autos were
crushed; fences, said one resident, "floated in the air like
paper." A youth inside a garage died when it collapsed. All bus,
trolley, and railroad transportation halted. Pigeons, unable to
fly, were smashed against the windshields of automobiles. The
streets from Front to the foot of Asylum Hill were waterways.
But the 17-foot bronze statue atop the State Capitol dome,
called "The Genius of Connecticut," held firm. In total five people died and twenty-two were injured.

The river continued to rise, reaching 35.1 feet above normal, and the East Side, where small shopkeepers, still paying
on loans taken out after the 1936 flood, had to be evacuated.
Fortunately, this would be the last such disaster for the city,
since an elaborate system of new dikes had already been
started and would be completed in 1941. The other major
rivers in the state, the Housatonic, the Thames, and the Naugatuck, rose to new levels.

Above Hartford, in Windsor, 3,000 acres of shade-grown
tobacco were ruined. More than twenty sheds filled with the
season's crop were swept downstream. Trees on the town
green that had stood since the American Revolution were
strewn about like jackstraws.

Eastern Connecticut was not spared. Willimantic, its roads
blocked with tree trunks, faced isolation when the Bolton
Notch Dam burst, pouring millions of gallons of water into the
crippled area. Those in marooned buildings used white birch

bark on the roofs to form pleas for help. Nearby Columbia paid its toll in apple trees; in Lucius Robinson's orchard one hundred trees fell and 1,000 bushels rotted. Farther east, the textile plants in Yantic and Fitchville were paralyzed. The Yantic River hurled tons of water against the bridge span and left it twisted. The wind wrenched loose the church steeple and dashed it to earth 50 feet away amidst a tangle of broken trees. At Fitchville the river disemboweled the three-story Palmer Brothers mill; pipes, beams, and machinery overhung the stream. In Norwich the surging Quinebaug River reached the ceilings of stores. Grocery stores were forced to ration food for several days. The chimney atop the five-story Wauregan Hotel crashed through its glass dome into the lobby. The Thames River dumped boats onto the streets. Franklin Square was under 12 feet of water.

In summary the U.S. Weather Bureau estimated the state's total property damage at over $100 million. The fishing industry took a terrible beating: fifty-three of Stonington's fifty-five-ship fleet were irreparable. In addition to New London and Hartford, the six-town coastal area suffered losses of at least $7 million. Other hard-hit towns were Manchester, Rockville, New Britain, Putnam, New Haven, Greenwich, Stamford, Norwalk, and Middletown. Yet the loss of eighty-five lives, in view of the hurricane's extent and intensity, was a remarkably low number.

A THREE-RING HORROR

The Hartford Circus Fire

1944

It was the worst human-caused disaster in Connecticut, occurring at the height of World War II in Hartford. The death toll was 168, mostly women and children who perished in its first ten minutes.

By Thursday, July 6, 1944, the Ringling Brothers Barnum & Bailey Circus had arrived in the city to set up its large tent on Barbour Street for its annual spectacular. It was a warm day, with a strong southwesterly breeze, perfect for mothers and fathers to take excited youngsters to enjoy an afternoon of fun.

Under the oil-impregnated canvas, 6,000 fans applauded an animal act. Just as the lions were herded back into the runway cages and the Flying Wallendas ascended to the high wire, it happened. Fifty feet from the main entrance was a four-sided canvas screen for the men's toilet. A man inside carelessly tossed his cigarette butt onto the ground. In seconds a flame crept up one side of the partition and licked at the guy ropes. One of the Wallendas pointed to the blaze from his perch above and yelled, "The tent's on fire!"

Ushers ran to the fast-spreading flames with buckets of water, but the fire was already beyond control. Momentarily, there was quiet and a few exhortations to keep calm and move slowly. Then, as the band continued playing as loudly as it could, someone screamed, panic erupted, and the crowd began stampeding toward the exits. Flaming pieces of canvas fell into the multitude, igniting hair and clothes. Ropes burned through and dropped heavy trapeze equipment into the center of the arena. The big tent poles crashed. At one exit a circus attendant inexplicably held back the surging mob. Scores of others, unable to climb over the steel animal runways, were knocked down and trampled to death, their bodies discovered later when the firemen were wetting down the ruins.

Many fought their way to the top tier of seats, where they leapt 15 feet to the ground or slid down the poles and ropes. Police Commissioner Edward J. Hickey, shepherding his nine nieces and nephews, was one who tossed his charges to safety. Those who dashed from the grandstand to the floor, desperately pushing chairs aside, soon realized there was no escape through the jammed exits, turned back, and climbed to the top.

Meanwhile, an animal trainer had the presence of mind to grab a whip and drive two lions still in the runway cage back to their wagon. Chris A. Hoffman, a seventy-one-year-old retired New York fire captain, had just guided his family safely along the runway to the cages. He saw Mazy Kovar, in charge of four leopards, standing in the cage with the fire roaring above her; an old man grabbed a hose and "I jumped in and gave him a hand [as] she stood there so calm and level-headed, telling us to direct the water on the animals."

"Hair raising" was the way twelve-year-old Jimmy Ahearn, of West Hartford, described his experience. He found himself

Just ten minutes after the Hartford circus fire began, 139 were already dead.
CONNECTICUT HISTORICAL SOCIETY MUSEUM

stranded amid a chaotic throng with his eight-year-old sister
Judy. "When we saw the blaze start near the entrance, I decided
just to stay put. I figured the crowd would stampede and we
would be safer in our seat." Finally, a way opened up for them
to slip down a passageway and crawl out under the side flaps.

Another survivor was Billy S. Garvie, a seventy-six-year-old nationally known authority on the circus who had attended every Ringling Brothers show in Hartford since 1900. Before the matinee, he chatted with George Smith, the manager, watching the crowd enter:

> I never saw so many women and little children in my life. War work kept the fathers away. . . . It was a sellout. I went to my seat in the front row of Section C. I was on the southwest side, the sunny side where the wind was coming from, near the main entrance. The animal acts just finished and the Wallendas were shoving off on the high wire when somebody yelled 'Fire!' I looked toward the entrance and saw the upper part of the side wall blazing. It was a patch of red flame about 10 feet square, but from there it traveled fast up and to both sides all at once. The fire at first was 40 feet away, but the wind drove it at us, cutting us off from the entrance. I climbed over the rail into the crowd moving down the track to the performers' entrance, south side. It was a mass mob, shouting and jostling but keeping on the move. The band played all the time I was in the crowd leaving, which was not more than five minutes. A woman from South Windsor had both arms burned to the shoulder, the skin hanging like empty sleeves. She cried that her three children were lost.

Hundreds apparently owed their lives to thirteen-year-old Donald Anderson, of Columbia, and his jackknife. He was there with his uncle, Alex Carlson, who told him to save himself if they got separated. The small boy got out by wriggling under the sidewall canvas, but he knew others couldn't follow because of their size and age. He whipped out his knife and slit the canvas along the sidewall as fast as possible. What made his feat special was the fact that Donald had a handicap. He walked with a cane, one of his legs being shorter than the other. Unable to play baseball or football, he always carried the knife for whittling; his treasured possession made him a hero.

Another hero, the son of a policeman, was Timothy Moynihan, only ten years old. He and nine friends were sitting on the topmost row of the bleachers. When the fire broke out, he started to run down the stairs, but a soldier told him "don't run, take it easy." Coolly, he returned to his seat; then, his way blocked, he jumped 15 feet to the ground. Lifting up one corner of the canvas, he beckoned others to follow. Eight of his friends made it. After assisting two dozen persons to safety, he ran across the street to the nearest telephone. When his father answered, he said, "I'm safe, Dad, don't worry."

Two soldiers injured in action overseas had been sent back to an army rest camp. They were given tickets to the circus for relaxation. Though receiving first aid for minor injuries sustained while escaping from the Big Top, they stood by and helped carry out bodies and people severely injured.

The strong wind swept the inferno across the top of the tent. In ten minutes on that sultry afternoon in 1944, 139 died and 225 were seriously burned.

In the field outside milled the terrified, disheveled survivors: parents running to and fro looking for lost children, shocked rescuers carrying blackened little bodies, some still alive, some not. Emergency aid was quickly mobilized. Several of the larger factories engaged in war work sent equipment and personnel. The Colt Armory dispatched four ambulances, four doctors, eight nurses, and twenty guards.

Victims were rushed to the hospitals. Mayor William Mortensen toured the wards of the municipal hospital. "The scene was heartbreaking," he said. Scores of persons, 142 in all, mostly children, lay horribly burned on hospital beds, while doctors and nurses hovered around, most of whom had never treated third-degree burns before. One child died as the mayor walked by. Her face drawn with the pain of her burns and tears filling her eyes.

Marion Dineen of Hartford, a fourteen-year-old blonde, had gone to the circus with her uncle, a cousin, and her eight-year-old brother.

> As the fire started, we sat for a moment expecting it was a little thing and they would have it out in a minute. Then I heard somebody yell "fire" and I grabbed hold of my brother Billy. I dropped his hand to go over the animal cage and caught my foot there, but I yanked my foot out of my shoe and went on over. Then I ran toward a door, and I haven't seen my brother.

Billy was listed among the dead, trapped behind the animal chute just a few seconds before it collapsed.

Shirley Snelgrove, of Plainville, had gone to the circus with her parents to celebrate her thirteenth birthday. Lying in bed, she told her story:

> We were having a birthday party, mother, father, and I. The fire started opposite us. I saw it right away and the three of us went up to the top of the bleachers. But we lost our nerve to jump and thought we'd try the main entrance. Mother and father went across the animal cages but I couldn't get

across them. So then I got separated from them and went back to the top of the bleachers. I jumped then. They dragged me from under the tent and I walked across the street and sat on the lawn.

Taken to the hospital suffering burns on her arms, legs, and back, she agonized over the fate of her parents. They both had died.

The State Armory drill shed was hastily converted into a morgue. Of 127 bodies delivered, 15 were still unidentified the next morning. Two detectives, Thomas Doyle and Edward Lowe, were especially affected by the body of a six-year-old, honey-haired child. Family after family looking for loved ones passed by her cot. No one claimed her. Perhaps her parents had also died. She was buried in Northwood Cemetery. Lt. Thomas C. Barber and Sgt. Edward T. Lowe brought flowers to decorate the grave of "Little Miss 1565" every July 6, Memorial Day, and Christmas for the rest of their lives.

By 5 P.M. all that remained of the circus were acres of ashes from seventeen tons of flammable canvas and a grandstand in ruins. Early Saturday, the eighty-car, red-and-yellow circus train was allowed to depart for Sarasota, its headquarters, where it was reequipped. At the end of July it resumed its itinerary, first in Akron, Ohio. The big tent was gone forever; henceforth performances were given in ballparks and stadiums.

While the injured recovered slowly in the hospitals, the *Hartford Times* started a disaster fund. From all over the state $56,000 poured in to the Red Cross for disbursement to those most in need. Inevitably, the conflagration launched several investigations and led to arrests and a host of claims. On January 11, 1945, the coroner released his report, a lengthy document

A clown with a bucket of water rushes to help. CONNECTICUT HISTORICAL SOCIETY MUSEUM

that placed the blame not on the anonymous careless smoker (or, as some claimed later, a crazed arsonist) but on the tent itself and the circus staff for significant failures. The traditional method of waterproofing the canvas tent was a disaster waiting to happen. The previous winter, it had been treated with an application of highly flammable white gasoline and paraffin, heated to the boiling point and then sprinkled with water.

But the disaster might not have happened in Hartford if the bosses and workers had followed their usual procedures. The boss canvasman, Leonard S. Aylesworth, had gone to Springfield that morning to prepare for the circus's next visit and left no one in charge. Though thirty-seven extinguishers were available, none had been placed inside. Outside stood four water wagons that were never manned. The usual NO SMOKING signs had not been posted. And so on.

The next month, on February 16, 1945, six men who had been arrested were tried in Superior Court. Three top officials—James A. Haley, the vice president, who usually traveled with the circus; George W. Smith, general manager; and Aylesworth, in charge of the big top—were found guilty of "involuntary manslaughter" and sentenced to prison for terms of two to seven years. A lot of political and business pressure ensued to stay their imprisonment. The circus president, Robert Ringling, hoped they could continue the road tour because "it would be impossible to replace them." As a result none served more than a year.

At the same time lawyers for the claimants swarmed forth, first attaching the circus train; but after the owners filed a $1 million bond, the attachment was lifted. There were so many of both lawyers and claimants that, through the intervention of the Hartford Bar Association, they agreed on June 24, in order to protect Ringling Brothers assets, to submit the 629 claims to a board of arbitration. Judge John H. King appointed Edward S. Rogin, a West Hartford attorney, as receiver. The arbitrators awarded a total of $3,946,000. The awards were all paid, but not until October 31, 1954.

In his 1944 annual report, Mayor Mortensen, who was also general manager of the Bushnell Memorial Hall, wrote: "The nation has a right to expect that we, in Hartford, the seat of so many great insurance firms, should develop from the crucible of our dread experience model laws for the protection of this and all other communities against similar tragedy." In January 1945 the Board of Aldermen adopted an ordinance providing for public safety at outdoor events and rigid inspection by the police, fire, and building departments. A year after the disaster, the Bureau of Standards in Washington approved a set of safety measures such as fire-resistant canvas and adequate entrances and exits.

On July 6, 2005, a $125,000 Circus Fire Memorial, designed by DuBose Associates and TO Design, was dedicated in the park behind Wish School. A bronze disk at the original location of the tent's center pole features the names of the 168 fatal victims.

THE SNEAKY SUPER STORM

Hurricanes
Connie and Diane
1955

After the Great Hurricane of 1938, Connecticut experienced two others, one in September 1944, and another in November 1944, but then none until August 31, 1954, when "Carol" struck the Old Saybrook–New London area with gusts up to 125 miles per hour and caused $50 million in property damage. But these were relatively minor compared with what the state had to face in 1955 from the torrential rains that fell during hurricanes "Connie" and "Diane." They resulted in the greatest natural disaster ever to occur in Connecticut, with total losses exceeding those of the 1936 flood and the 1938 hurricane.

Following a different pattern from previous hurricanes, Connie had sneaked up the Atlantic Coast from Cape Hatteras through Pennsylvania and into the Great Lakes, sparing the state from wind but not 3 to 8 inches of rain on August 12–13, 1955. It caused major flood damage in the southwestern part and set the stage for Hurricane Diane's arrival five days later, on August 18, from Maryland and New Jersey. Diane was wicked, inundating the Naugatuck Valley, the northwestern towns, and even east in Suffield, Putnam, and Stafford Springs (due to the collapse of the Quinebaug Dam in Southbridge, Massachusetts) with up to 16 inches of rain and causing 70 deaths, 4,700 injuries, and hundreds of millions in property damages.

Calling the floods "the worst disaster in the state's history," the governor, Abraham Ribicoff, immediately declared a state of emergency and asked President Eisenhower for federal assistance. Shortly after 1 A.M. on August 19, Eisenhower mobilized the National Guard. Throughout the state entire communities were isolated as raging water cut off roads, crumbled dozens of bridges, swept away railroad tracks, toppled houses, destroyed factories, and ruined supplies of drinking water and food stuffs. At least four major dams broke on Friday. The State Highway Department reported the destruction of at least seventeen bridges and the blocking of numerous roads by rock slides.

This was one of the first times helicopters played a major role in civilian rescue operations. Placed at the governor's disposal, he turned them over to Maj. Gen. Frederick B. Reincke, state adjutant general, who directed Maj. Gen. George B. Stanley, chief of the air staff, to assign priority missions. Just after 1 A.M., the U.S. Navy flew in the first sixteen; sixteen more were provided the next day. Specially equipped, these helicopters flew into the worst hit areas and took people off rooftops and out of trees. Three National Guard C-47s also arrived Friday to drop food to stricken communities.

Late Friday a First Army helicopter flying over Winsted reported that the entire business district and nearly all of the factories had been destroyed. From another helicopter Lt. Col. Robert Schwolsky of the National Guard said, "I've never seen anything like the Main Street. It looks like someone had taken cars and thrown them at one another." He saw a four-story building turned on its base and countless persons stranded on rooftops. After reports of looting, troops were rushed in.

The Naugatuck Valley, comprising Naugatuck, Ansonia, Seymour, Waterbury, and Torrington, was completely underwater. It was the first time that Waterbury had flooding in its business district. Mayor Raymond Snyder of Waterbury reported he saw at least a dozen bodies floating down the swollen Naugatuck River. The city's two largest manufacturers, American Brass and Scovill, were shut down with 15 feet of water inside their facilities. Torrington, a city of 28,000, was totally isolated for two days before help arrived. Several small businesses located in the city's center had become piles of debris. Center Street Bridge, a cement structure, was lifted in one piece, turned sideways, and deposited 100 feet downstream intact. The Torrington Company plant wasn't bailed out for a month, and the windows of the American Brass factory were pierced by thousands of lengths of lumber from the nearby Hotchkiss Lumber Company.

Twelve helicopters from Sikorsky were able to rescue 297 persons. When Lt. Calvin Rupp and copilot Richard Case sighted one marooned house, Rupp lowered himself to the roof, chopped a hole, and pulled five elderly persons out. From another helicopter its pilots, Lance Ellis and Dale Paulis, saw three men standing on a partially sunken house top. One, holding a cat in his arms, yelled, "I'm too scared to get into the helicopter but please take the cat!" His companion hit him with a hard right to the jaw and then the men and cat were soon winging their way to safety. Pilots James Ferguson and Lt. Cdr. Russell Bowers rescued eight people on six hoists; two were women clutching babies in their arms. TV antennas presented a big problem. The pilots soon learned that by hovering to one side and gunning the engine, the backlash would topple them. After their long day of saving lives, the pilots also agreed that "despite loss of homes and belongings, [those rescued] showed wonderful spirit."

Those living in the River Glen section along the Farmington River were especially affected. In one incident a state police boat evacuating a house capsized, and two children in it were swept away in full view of their parents and horrified spectators. At about 4 A.M. the William Davis family had been warned to leave their home. As they packed their clothes and valuables, the water reached the first floor, and then went higher. Mr. Davis broke a hole through the roof. As he was helping out his two young sons, they were torn away by a wall of water, and both Mr. and Mrs. Davis were swept nearly 5 miles by the roaring torrent before being able to cling to trees. Seven hours later, they were saved, only to learn that their son and their new tenants on the second floor drowned when the Davis home was demolished.

Two Farmington firemen rescued another family, but the rescue boat swamped. Swept along by the current, the parents and three children managed to cling to the roof of a submerged house; they tied their children to trees, got ashore, and flagged down a helicopter that picked up the mother and one child. Her second child was saved from the tree, but the third, unable to hold on, drowned. Two Goose Bay, Labrador, pilots flying a large H 21 helicopter out of Westover Field in Massachusetts, were able to swoop down and lift aboard a thirteen-year-old girl polio victim from a flood-stalled ambulance. She was taken to a Hartford hospital.

This 1955 Myers Studio photo shows hurricane damage on Main Street in Unionville, looking upsteam. CONNECTICUT HISTORICAL SOCIETY MUSEUM

One incident that just escaped being a tragedy involved a Farmington volunteer fireman named Albert Leone and a pretty, five-year-old girl, Yolanda Bartolomeo. Before dawn on Friday, Leone and another fireman, Edward Durant, had evacuated her by boat along with her mother, three young siblings, and pet beagle from their tiny River Glen home. The boat swamped almost at once, but all seven managed to clamber on to a rooftop. After tying the children to trees, the adults flagged a helicopter that hauled Mrs. Bartolomeo and two of the children aboard. Just as the others were about to be pulled in, the house broke loose from its foundations. Durant and Joseph, age fourteen, clung to a tree. Leone decided to tie Yolanda to another tree before he was torn away, crying "Wait for me Yolanda. I'll be back." He swam 4 miles before making dry land in the back of the Winchell Smith flour mill. Hurrying back to the firehouse, he got a second helicopter to search in vain for the other members of the family. Late in the afternoon, a rescue boat picked up Durant and Joseph. Yolanda and her little dog were still missing as darkness fell. At 5 A.M. Saturday, a man named Walter Balazy set out in his canoe. Six hours later he found Yolanda playing in the sandy rubble with her dog. She had untied herself from the tree. Her first words were, "What happened to Mr. Leone?" She was suffering from mild shock, but was chipper.

Normally peaceful brooks and streams became raging torrents. In Simsbury, Hop Brook flowed from west to east through the grounds and brownstone buildings of the Ensign-Bickford Company, makers of safety fuses, there since 1836. It wreaked havoc even before the Farmington River backed up to deal the firm a second blow from the east. The same river dealt severe blows to Collinsville; though the dam there held, the highway bridge below it, carrying all the traffic between Hartford and Torrington, fell. In the village the picturesque Collins Company, world famous for the manufacture of axes and machetes, lost two of its many shops.

Scores of telephones were manned at the Connecticut State Police barracks in Hartford. The information received was relayed to disaster headquarters at the State Armory, which directed the operation of rescue equipment. Many of the calls that swamped the police operators made them throw up their hands in disgust. A West Hartford woman called to say there was water in her basement, and what could she do about it. An Avon farmer asked for an LST boat to evacuate his one hundred cows from a flooded pasture. Others wanted to know when it would stop raining. Troopers returning to the barracks after spending the day in flooded areas had bizarre stories to tell. One reported seeing a house, complete with lawn and landscaping, floating down the river.

Not only the highways but also the railroads paid a heavy price. The New Haven Railroad reported twenty-four washouts, six landslides, one five-car derailment of a freight train, ten bridges gone, and considerable damage to tracks. At Waterbury the freight yard was submerged; a yard office floated away along with forty boxcars that were lifted off their wheel trucks. In Avon a crew was rescued by boat when their train became trapped between two washouts.

But no town or village in the path of the "Super Sneaky Storm" suffered more than the industrial city of Winsted, with its population of 11,000. Main Street, better known as Route 44, was a river 14 feet deep. Seven dead. No drinking water, gas, or sewer system, some electric power, as many as 1,500 without homes, 300 automobiles destroyed. Total damages in excess of $27 million.

Riding on one of the National Guard's amphibious "ducks," Evans Clinchy, a staff writer for the *Hartford Times,* was one of the first observers to reach Winsted, arriving at 4 P.M. Friday.

The flood apparently took the town by surprise even though advance notice was spread through Thursday night. Private James Bolio, a Marine home on leave, said that he had helped local and state police try to clear the main street. Many people simply refused to leave the area, even though they were told the flood was coming.

The main street looked as if a bulldozer and dynamite crew had come along and simply blown up everything in sight. . . . The entire road, running from one end of town to the other, has been dug out by the flood to a depth of four to five feet. The town is completely split down the middle . . . and cut almost totally from the world outside.

The only line of communication is by short wave military radio or by helicopter. The Connecticut National Guard is flying a regular helicopter run every hour or so, bringing in medical supplies, guard reinforcements, water purifying equipment, and electric generators.

In another eyewitness account, on August 23, James Devlin, an Associated Press journalist, wrote:

The water was gone now and the havoc showed in naked detail. For a mile and a half aptly-named Mad River had ripped up the asphalt pavement of Main Street and flooded and destroyed the stores along its route. It was as though a drunken giant had run a huge plow the length of the business section, leaving a trail of boulders, sand, gravel, broken paving, and precipitous ditches.

Salvage and cleanup operations are going forward as fast as possible, but there still has not been time to clear all the groceries of rotted and spoiled food. The flies gather and at night so do rats. But the flood has had its compensations, not the least of which is a new comradery among the people.

Just as the novelist and Pulitzer Prize winner John Hersey had brought home the stark tragedy of what an atomic bomb did to the city of Hiroshima, so he told through interviews the story of the disaster inflicted by nature, not by man, in Winsted. The events he described in the August 28 edition of the *Hartford Courant* took place mostly on the flat roofs of two one-story buildings at the lower end of the dangerous mile later dubbed "Hurricane Rapids." It was about 5:30 A.M., and the men of Volunteer Fire Company #3 were on high ground on Oak Street. For hours they'd heard a man and woman screaming for help from the second floor of a tenement building and signaling with a flashlight. It turns out the pair were a brother and sister, Joe and Maria Cornelia, who had arrived from Italy two weeks before the storm.

> Whole buildings had begun to give way . . . and boards and refrigerators and clothes were coursing down what had now become rapids eight feet deep. . . . The debris from the houses that had fallen was striking the tenement block where the Cornelios were stranded.

The firemen worked their way to a wide platform facing the Cornelios but about 80 feet from them. For three-quarters of an hour they tried to get a rope over. When that didn't work, Dewey Plank ran home for his spinner rod.

> The cast looked impossible. The cloudburst was still falling. The wind was strong. There was a maze of telephone and light wires just above and in front of the Cornelios' windows. He cast once. He was badly short. . . . After half a dozen casts his lure caught on a telephone pole near the windows, and with a broom Joseph Cornelio drew in the line.

A rescue boat arrived, but it looked like the whole tenement block would be washed away. Time was short.

> Steve Jackson, 35, pulled himself up to the window, put a leather mackinaw on Maria Cornelio, and tied a line under her arms and let her down to the boat. He let her brother down the same way. . . . Halfway across Maria Cornelio panicked, grabbed the main rope, stood up. The boat capsized. . . . All five fell in the river. All were lashed to the boat. . . . Maria Cornelio threw her arms overhead and her rope slipped off. As she floated away, Joe Horte grabbed her and his rope broke and the pair were borne swiftly away. . . . Maria Cornelio fought, broke away, screamed, and drowned.

It was afternoon. The rain had stopped. All the rescuers went to Officer Ferris Resha's family restaurant and had their first food and drink in eighteen hours.

A NEW YEAR'S EVE NIGHTMARE

The Cathedral Fire
1956

December 31, 1956, was a cold, snowy Monday. At the top of the Hotel Bond, in the ballroom, the Hartford Rotary Club had just adjourned its weekly meeting at 1:30 P.M. I was standing on the dais looking out the large window along Farmington Avenue to the west. I saw a column of black smoke rising high into the sky. Looking closely, I exclaimed, "St. Joseph's Cathedral is on fire!" Already, the center was in flames; only the two brownstone towers, each with four spires, stood. Not until later did I learn that the fire had started after the 7:00 mass.

For three hours only smoke was visible. By 11:00 the entire structure, the center of worship for Catholics of the Archdiocese of Hartford, had become a raging furnace when a large chunk of the ceiling over the main altar broke through. Two groups of firemen, battling blazes behind the altar, heard a sharp, cracking sound echo through the vaulted auditorium half filled with smoke. Minutes before, another squad of firemen had been on the roof of the sacristy area; two had been overcome by smoke and lowered to the ground by rope.

Like a cyclone, flames covered the roof and erupted through the large rose windows on three sides. A massive ball of fire shot hot embers across the avenue to the grounds of the Aetna Life Insurance Company. Smoke billowed 1,000 feet into the air. Three gold crosses on three sides melted and hung from the towers. "When the flames broke through, then we lost her," Fire Chief Henry G. Thomas said later.

When it was evident the entire interior would go, the adjoining buildings of the cathedral complex were ordered evacuated: the rectory, chancery, community hall, parochial elementary school, and the Sisters of Mercy Convent.

Amazingly, the conflagration was the second to strike a Catholic church in the city within a day. Early Christmas morning, the venerable brownstone St. Patrick's downtown had been ravaged by a three-alarm fire, which burned out a large part of the roof and most of the steeple. Many stained-glass windows were also shattered by the heat. Chief Thomas was convinced that the two fires so close together "have to be more than coincidence." Hartford's mayor, Joseph W. Cronin, agreed. It looked like arson.

Because of the St. Patrick's fire, cathedral staff had taken the precaution of searching the buildings Sunday night and then locking the doors until 6:30 A.M., when they were opened for the morning Mass. During Mass the Reverend Francis S. O'Neill had smelled smoke, and as soon as he had finished he hurried into the sacristy. James McSweegan, the deputy fire chief, who had been attending the Mass, was already there. "I think, Father, it's coming from the basement." Frank Macken, the cathedral's engineer, had pulled the fire alarm at 7:33 A.M. When firemen arrived, smoke was beginning to billow from the basement under the altar, filling the main church with a thick haze.

At its height 300 firemen, including men from three surrounding towns, worked to control the fire. The injuries were minor. Two firemen hurt their backs when a ceiling in the basement fell on them. A department captain, John A. O'Reilly, was struck in the eye by a burning ember. Three firemen were overcome by smoke. Later, Fire Marshal George F. Kennedy, forty-two, at St. Francis Hospital, his lungs so filled with smoke he was hardly able to speak, said, "What a kick that fire was." Edward F. Steimach had been working on the roof with a dozen other firemen chopping holes. "That smoke was so thick you could have smoked a ham up there!" Another fireman had to be removed from the roof by aerial ladder and taken to St. Francis Hospital. Altogether, ten were hurt. Miraculously, no one was killed.

The Metropolitan District estimated that the firemen poured close to 1,500,000 gallons of water into the cathedral. The Salvation Army rushed to the scene at 8:45 A.M. with its mobile canteen unit and twelve workers, distributing hot beef stew, coffee, and doughnuts. They also handed out work gloves and stockings to the soaked men. The Aetna Life cafeteria set up another stand with hot coffee and food. Neighboring churches, Bushnell Memorial Hall, and the Statler Hotel offered their facilities for worship. So did the State Armory.

Police Chief Michael J. Godfrey said it was the worst fire he had seen in his thirty-seven years of experience. He wasted no time starting an investigation. Scores of detectives began combing the area to question people. By one o'clock he had arranged for a twenty-four-hour guard on all the churches in the city. Seven men were picked up and two of them held for questioning. One suspect had been overheard in a drugstore saying, "Don't get excited, it's only a church fire." Another had been seen three times trying to get into a Baptist church; he told the police that the priests and nuns should commit suicide. Though the local and state police mounted a thorough investigation, they were never able to pin down the disaster as arson.

In the early afternoon, the fire towers were still throwing tons of water into the shattered cathedral. Hose lines, snaking across Farmington and Asylum Avenues, caused a tremendous traffic jam. The water rushed back out of the burned building, forming what looked like a lake in front. Only the walls and two towers stood. All the beautiful stained-glass windows were gone. As were the rotunda, covered with $100,000 worth of gold leaf, and the great organ.

The police pushed back hundreds of spectators to keep them safe from falling embers. "What'll I do? She was in the church," pleaded a man cradling a shivering alley-variety cat, its fur matted from the water. A minister holding a bag of groceries stared silently; his wife tugged at his sleeve. "Let's go," she said. "It's frightful. They'll never save it now." Many of Aetna's 3,000 employees watched from the windows of the largest colonial-style office building in the world. No one could believe it happened. One observer said, "It looks like one of the bombed out churches in Europe."

On Tuesday thousands of Roman Catholics attended early masses at the State Armory and the Allyn Theater.

It had taken sixteen years to build Saint Joseph's. It was consecrated in 1892. The land on which it stood had belonged to the family of J. Pierpont Morgan, who was born in Hartford. Early Gothic in style, it had seventy-two stained-glass windows that came from Innsbruck, Germany. Its high altar of marble rose three stories. In the chancel was the carved oak bishop's throne. It could seat 2,000. Only a pitifully small amount of church valuables were saved. When smoke began pouring into the nave, a rescue brigade of policemen, firemen, and priests had moved up and down the aisles, carrying out all the gold chalices, crucifixes, cassocks, and other articles they could. They barely had time to rip loose an 18-by-30-foot Oriental rug and drag it outside. It was obvious that the insurance coverage of $3 million would be woefully inadequate to replace the loss of building and contents.

For Archbishop Henry J. O'Brien, in particular, the fire was a bitter blow. Only three years after his consecration, he had become a well-liked leader of the 600,000 faithful in the metropolitan area and had taken an active interest in the affairs of Hartford. On Friday, January 4, he publicly expressed

> profound gratitude for assistance given during and after the fire. . . . A disaster like this seems at first to be wholly without good points. But in a very short space of time, the good points begin to appear and to console us. One of them is a community's drawing together in a family spirit of common concern and united effort.

One of the archbishop's closest friends was Morgan Brainard, chairman of Aetna Life, who was regarded as the city's "godfather." Three years before, the company had celebrated its one hundredth anniversary and in 1955 Brainard's half-century of employment. Wags said that on one side of Farmington Avenue, Aetna insured you before death, and on the other side, the Catholics insured you after death. On the day of the fire, Morgan rushed across the street to console Archbishop O'Brien. "Bishop," he said, "I want to offer you our auditorium for church services next Sunday. Also, since I'm vitally interested in what happens to Farmington Avenue, I would like to have something to say about the architecture of the new cathedral I'm sure you will build." Unsaid was Morgan's wish to have a colonial-style building to complement his domain. The archbishop warmly accepted the offer but shook his head over the last remark. "Morgan, I have no control over what will be built. You'll have to speak to Cardinal Spellman in New York."

Without delay Morgan arranged a luncheon with Cardinal Spellman at the prestigious 21 Club in New York City. After consuming several martinis, they discussed the design of the new cathedral, two potentates unwilling to yield an inch of turf. Finally, the cardinal asked what building Aetna's chairman liked best next to his own. Morgan named the modern National Fire Insurance on Asylum Avenue (now part of the St. Francis Hospital and Medical Center). "All right," conceded Spellman, "I will agree to hire the same architect and builder."

The modern, beautiful, towering, stone cathedral was dedicated in 1962. Among its outstanding features are a white marble altar, a gigantic ceramic mural of Christ in Glory, and French stained-glass windows.

MEDICAL CENTER MALADY

The Hartford Hospital Fire

1961

In older convalescent homes the danger of fire is always prevalent. Connecticut's worst such fire happened on Christmas Eve in 1945 at Hartford's Niles Street Hospital, claiming the lives of twenty-one elderly residents. Adequate fire protection is expected of large hospitals, with their hundreds of patients of all ages, so it was a great shock when, near another Christmas, Hartford's oldest medical center suffered a major disaster.

On Friday, December 8, 1961, fire raged out of control for nearly an hour through the ninth floor of the twelve-story Hartford Hospital. Of the sixteen who died from either smoke inhalation or burns, seven were patients, five visitors, two female employees, and a nurse and a doctor. The first alarm came in at 2:39 P.M. Fire Chief Thomas E. Lee arrived at the scene in a few minutes and immediately called in two more alarms. Dense billows of smoke poured out of the ninth-floor windows. Lee then ordered all 793 patients to be evacuated.

On the ninth floor Sonia Sandner, a nurse supervisor, was making her rounds when she saw a puff of smoke billow out from the rubbish chute. At once she closed the fire door and told the other nurses to shut the doors to patients' rooms. But smoke and flame burst out from the top of the chute and raced along the ceiling of the corridor. Sonia then descended to the lower floors to check the fire doors there. As firemen battled smoke and flames on the upper floors, patients leaned out the windows and screamed for help. On the eighth floor doctors shouted at patients to lie on the floor and keep the doors to their rooms closed.

Mrs. Barbara Valbona was visiting on the ninth floor. A nurse came by and shut the door.

> I heard an explosion, looked out and saw the fire. Someone came in. A lot of black smoke came through. I shut the door, put a wet sheet over it, opened the windows, and had every-body lie down on the floor. There were five of us. It was a four-bed ward. This is the second fire for me. I was in the circus fire when I was a kid.

Theodore Bisi described his experience:

> I went from the second to the ninth floor in the elevator. You could smell something like burning rags, but there was no smoke, and I didn't think much of it. We saw the flames as the attendant opened the elevator door. He closed it right away, we went up to the 11th and along the corridor to the wing of the hospital.

Those trapped in elevators kept in contact with the hospi-tal switchboard through the emergency telephone. Firemen battered down the steel doors to rescue them. Seven staff members en route to the ninth floor to fight the fire crawled out through the trap door in the ceiling of an elevator to an empty room on the tenth floor. Hearing a groan, Romeo Infante, a carpenter, crawled through the smoke to an exit, broke the window with his arm, cutting it badly (the cut was treated later), and pulled an unconscious man to safety. The man was revived and required no further help.

At the Central Fire Station urgent messages were relayed:

"We need a lot of help down here now. Get that new squad here!"

"Gas masks. We need gas masks."

"Need a ladder on the east side."

"We're still trying to get up. Still trying to get through the fire doors. They're shut."

"The elevators are out. We have to walk to the ninth floor."

"The smoke is clearing. A number of windows have been broken to ventilate the building."

"Call surrounding towns to bring ambulances to the Seymour side of the hospital."

"Ask the press to move their cars. They're blocking Seymour Street."

"We're dispatching a plane to help traffic."

"Traffic has let up in all locations. It's simmering down."

At 7 P.M. came the final dispatch: "We're picking up men at the hospital and heading back to the station. You all did a great job, men." Earlier, ninety town and company ambulances had arrived to take patients to eleven area hospitals which had offered 560 beds within an hour; some patients were transported to their homes.

Afterward, every witness stated that when they first saw smoke, they didn't think it serious, as they were used to fires in the rubbish chute and simply initiated the emergency fire procedures without calling the fire department. One of the first to discover the fire was Alfred LaFontaine, a maintenance man who had been in charge of cleaning the chute for eleven years. All kinds of rubbish were dumped: blood bottles, ether, paper, flower boxes. He had checked and cleaned the ninth-floor chute before lunch on that day. Later, he went to the ground floor and opened the chute door. "It looked like an atom bomb," he said. Flame and smoke roared out. He raced to the main floor, grabbed a fire hose, and poured water down the chute. But it was too late to save the ninth floor.

On Saturday Leo J. Mulcahy, the state police commissioner, and also state fire marshal, conducted a formal investigation. Fire officials testified that the building was fire resistant. State building codes didn't require sprinklers in such buildings except in hazardous areas. Marcella MacDonald, assistant head nurse, then spoke up; she was the one who pulled the box alarm at 2:39 P.M.

> I was walking down the corridor of the 12th floor when I noticed black smoke coming from the rubbish chute. I had a feeling it was a serious fire. I called a male aide over and told him to put tape around the edges of the chute door to keep the smoke out. I've been here 10 years and I've never pulled a fire alarm box in my life.

By Sunday Hartford Hospital was operating as usual, if somberly. Dr. Stewart Hamilton, medical director, said that "it was remarkable [the fire] was confined to one area." Adding that every floor would soon be in full operation except for the 108 beds on the ninth floor, he praised evacuated patients for their "uncomplaining fortitude" and employees "who stayed on duty and performed their tasks and many extra duties with calmness."

Still to be determined were what caused such a violent fire in the chute, and why the chute door blew out. After a four-hour meeting, state and local officials felt they had the answers. They suspected that some hospital employee had dumped a batch of highly flammable discarded X-ray film under the false impression it would not burn. The blaze became so intense that it set off a fire sprinkler at the top of the chute, turned the cascading water into steam, and created a pressure that eventually burst through the ninth-floor door. Fire Chief Lee described as "bad engineering" the chute vent that was so small it couldn't discharge the back pressure fast enough, the "weak link in the chain" of metal running vertically from roof to basement. He permanently banned the use of trash chutes.

The Hartford Hospital fire had a heavy impact on the design and construction of future hospitals, hotels, and rooming houses. The fire marshal ordered such public institutions to use only non-combustible materials as was already required of schools. Another change adopted was a ban on smoking.

THE RESCUE OF A RIVER

Connecticut River Pollution

1965

In a documentary film called *The Long Tidal River,* Katharine Hepburn characterized the 410-mile Connecticut River as "the most beautifully landscaped cesspool in the world." She knew firsthand how badly it had been polluted for more than 150 years. While making the 1955 film *Summertime* in Venice, the script called for her to fall backward into the Grand Canal. Her director, the famous David Lean, demurred. "Kate," he said, "it's too dirty. We'll use your understudy."

"No," she replied, "you forget I was raised at the mouth of the Connecticut River."

When the Dutch explorer Adraien Block discovered the river in 1614, sailing upstream as far as the Enfield Falls, 60 miles from Long Island Sound, he observed that near what is now Hamburg Cove, the water became fresh, so he named the great river "de Versche." Immense schools of fish once populated the whole length—shad, salmon, striped bass, and sixty other species. Fishing was a principal source of food for the peaceful river Indians. They despised shad as good only for fertilizing their cornfields. Salmon were so plentiful in Colonial days that it was prohibited to feed them to bond servants more than three times weekly. Alas, the salmon run ended about 1800, doomed by the dams erected to provide waterpower for factories, which blocked passage to the salmon spawning grounds.

For 200 years, from 1650 to 1850, the river was a mainstay of trade and travel. By 1750 merchants in the Connecticut Valley had developed an extensive coastal and West Indian trade, filling the holds of their sloops and brigs with grain, onions, dried corn, horses, mules, lumber, barrel staves, and brownstone. Imports consisted mainly of sugar, molasses, coffee, salt, and—in greatest demand of all—hogsheads of rum for the thirsty colonists. Next to farming, shipbuilding employed the most workers and was the state's first important industry. Dozens of family-owned yards from Old Lyme to East Windsor accounted for an estimated 4,000 sailing vessels of all kinds by the time wind-powered transportation gave way to the railroad and the steamboat.

In 1854, having run out of ground water, the city of Hartford began pumping fresh water from the river up to Lord's Hill (now home of the Hartford Insurance Group). That year, a major flood inundated the city, the worst on record until 1936. Just twelve years later the water was no longer potable. Hartford, with a population of over 30,000, was still an active river port, handling 600,000 tons of cargo (mostly coal) and 26,000 passengers on the steamboats that ran regularly to and from New York. Large factories such as the Colt Armory, Weed Sewing Machine, and Woodruff & Beach discharged their waste directly into the Hog River, which had become a smelly, unsightly stream. The liberal preacher Horace Bushnell was perhaps Connecticut's first environmentalist; as early as 1854, he had persuaded the city fathers to purchase the area for a municipal park, dedicated in 1876. Previously, this area was in the city's worst slum, crowded with pig farms.

Finally, state officials began to take note of what was happening. In 1884 the chairman of the Board of Agriculture said, "Hartford sits nervously in the lap of what was once one of the fairest and sweetest and is now one of the filthiest valleys in the world." But industry ignored the impending disaster, saying the Park River emptying into the Connecticut "affords excellent facilities for sewage"—up and down the river. Paper mills in Vermont, manufacturers in Holyoke and Springfield, downriver towns like Middletown, none had treatment plants and were pouring raw sewage into the once-pristine waters of New England's longest body of water.

From the public viewpoint the river was an asset only as a convenient open sewer and a highway for cheap transportation. Too frequently, flooding made it a liability. Samuel Colt saw it differently. To protect the Colt Armory, at his own expense he constructed a dike nearly 2 miles long that protected the South Meadows for eighty years. Others ignored the filth and odors and continued to use the river for recreation in the summertime. The Hartford Yacht Club, organized in 1895, held annual regattas. But, generally speaking, the river was ignored, forgotten, and abused. The steamboats stopped running in 1931. River traffic was limited to barges bringing fuel oil to tank farms in Portland, Rocky Hill, and Wethersfield. With the construction of a 45-foot high dike in 1941, and the completion of Interstate 91 ten years later, Hartford had totally isolated itself from its waterfront.

The first 33 miles of the river, from Long Island Sound to Middletown, has always been cleaner and is still beautiful. First, it meanders through a floodplain on both sides, then changes character becoming wider and deeper, its banks covered with hemlock and oak, framed by gentle hills and rock ledges. Surprisingly, it is relatively unspoiled by development. There are two reasons: first, the sandbar at the mouth prevented Saybrook from becoming a major port like New London or New Haven. Secondly, most of the riverfront had for generations been privately owned. Were Adraien Block to return, he would still be able to admire the salty marshes, the migratory birds, the eminence of Joshua's Rock, the Middletown gorge, and the hills known as the Seven Sisters near Hadlyme, where the actor and playwright William Gillette built his stone castle. However, the estuary area did not escape pollution entirely; the use of DDT decimated osprey and marsh birds until banned.

The time had come to reverse man's predation. It began when in December 1963 Dr. Franklin M. Foote, the state health commissioner, declared at an environmental conference that for more than sixty years the Connecticut River had so high a coliform bacteria count as to be unsuitable for recreational use. That shocked the public. It had this official classification: "suitable for transportation of sewage and industrial wastes and for power, navigation and certain industrial uses." Then, in 1965 the *Long Tidal River* documentary was shown on TV. An instant success, it stirred up widespread concern and became a catalyst for launching a crusade for clean water. On October 7, Gov. John Dempsey appointed one hundred leading citizens to develop an action program. He chose Thomas F. Malone, head of research for Travelers Insurance Company, as chairman; Ellsworth S. Grant as vice chairman; and Richard Martin as

executive secretary. At the first meeting the governor empha-
sized that this group would not be just another study committee. "You are a task force called together to examine the
pollution that we know exists and tell us the best, quickest and
most efficient and economical way to eliminate it."

The magnitude of the problem to be solved was formida-
ble. Connecticut has forty-seven rivers and streams of various
lengths totaling 900 miles. In 1965 pollution of the fourteen
major waterways made all but a few miles unsuitable for
bathing, recreation, or fishing. Most of the municipal sewage
plants provided only primary treatment. Half of the industrial
wastes were untreated. For the cities and industries to install secondary treatment, which would remove 90 percent of the bad
stuff, would be the most expensive state program ever under-
taken, totaling as much as $250 million (today $2.5 billion).

The task force set May 1, 1966, as the target date for present-
ing its report. Working through ten subcommittees, it set out to
deal with various aspects of pollution and their effect on people
and wildlife. Progress toward a consensus was rapid and har-
monious with one exception: Some manufacturers objected to
the stringency of the recommended water quality standards
and placing the burden of proof for polluting on the polluter.
The 128-page report, containing thirty-two recommendations,
called for $150 million in bonds to finance the construction of
new water treatment plants. It proposed tax incentives to help
industry control its waste. (President Lyndon Johnson would
soon sign the federal Clean Waters Act that reduced the cost to
municipalities from 40 percent to 20 percent.)

The program had the full support of Governor Dempsey,
who stressed the importance of keeping the issue of clean
water, which affected the well-being of every resident, from

let's get one thing clear—WATER

Clean water is Connecticut's lifeblood. With it Connecticut has prospered. Without it Connecticut will fail. If we do not start now to improve our water quality, future generations will inherit a declining state with no industries and few jobs. That Connecticut's water has become foul is unmistakable. The stench of pollution hangs in the atmosphere. Our rivers and our streams are being described as "open sewer drains". Dead fish can often be seen rotting in our waterways. Oil and sewage threaten our beaches, both public and private. Long Island Sound is in danger of becoming little more than a large, tidal cesspool. The danger of disease, hepatitis, typhoid, dysentery, and many others, daily grows more real. The situation is critical.

WHAT CAN YOU DO for clearer, cleaner water necessary for recreation, drinking, industry and agriculture? Write for a copy of the report of the Clean Water Task Force for Connecticut:

Thomas F. Malone, Chairman

CLEAN WATER TASK FORCE FOR CONNECTICUT

Room 125A
State Office Building
Hartford, Conn.
06115

The Clean Water Task Force, established in October 1965, is a bi-partisan group of 100 people organized to formulate a plan of action to solve the water pollution problems of Connecticut. Their resulting four-step Action Program, containing 32 recommendations, deserves the active support of every citizen in the State.

let's
get
one
thing
clear—
WATER

This ad, created by Roger Eddy, former state senator, novelist, and Newington farmer, caught the public's attention during the clean water campaign.

becoming a partisan one. Dr. Malone appointed an action committee to undertake an intensive public relations campaign to
enlist voter support and pave the way for acceptance of the
report at the next session of the legislature. The theme: "Let's
Get One Thing Clear: Water!" The campaign met with a uni-
formly favorable reaction; even industry endorsed the goal of a
Class B rating, suitable for fish and wildlife habitat, recreational boating, swimming, and certain industrial processes.
But, as with every major bill involving a new government program and the expenditure of large sums, no one was sure of
legislative approval. The public hearing on House Bill 2417 ran
five hours. The *Hartford Courant* reported that "a Republican
drumbeat of criticism, preceded . . . by declarations of support
for 'the principle,' continued throughout the long hearing." Dr.
Malone countered by noting that the task force report had been
adopted unanimously by its one hundred members, "a group
that embraced every section of Connecticut's social, political
and economic structure—including conservationists and
industrialists."

It was a tense moment in the House on the day of the vote.
The gallery was filled with supporters holding their breath.
Then cheers and applause erupted as the bill was adopted without a single dissenting vote. The Clean Water Act was signed on
May 1. The governor said, "When future histories of Connecticut are written, I feel certain that 1967 will be marked as the
year when this state set an example for the rest of the country."

The Clean Water goals were not achieved as intended in
seven years, nor in ten years. By 1980, however, nearly half the
stream miles of the Connecticut River and its tributaries had
been restored to Class B. The river was swimmable from Middletown to its mouth. Shad, striped bass, even a few Atlantic

salmon returned in greater numbers. The osprey and bald eagle reappeared. In 1974 eight towns in the estuary area formed the Gateway Conservation Zone, an intertown compact to protect the undeveloped land bordering both sides. The same year, the Connecticut River Foundation was organized in Essex and restored the dock and warehouse of the old steamboat landing. Other towns like Middletown and Old Saybrook pitched in with riverside parks. Through conservation easements and outright donations to the state, and the efforts of local land trusts and private groups like the Nature Conservancy, hundreds of acres more were preserved.

The crowning achievement, as people rediscovered the river and were drawn to it in increasing numbers, was the formation in 1980 of Riverfront Recapture in Hartford under the sponsorship of the Travelers Insurance Company. That was the beginning of a twenty-year, multimillion-dollar project. Despite the obstacles of dike, railroad, and interstate highway, direct access to the riverfront was restored: two new parks, Charter Oak Landing (close to the location of the seventeenth-century Dutch trading post), and Great River Park in East Hartford; 6 miles of walking paths from the Charter Oak Bridge to Riverside Park; a plaza built across a lowered section of I–91; and the resurrection of Riverside Park by building a large boathouse. Today, Riverfront operates a dazzling variety of recreational and educational programs on the waterfront year-round, such as a big bass tournament, concerts on the plaza, steamboat rides, racing eight-oared shells, and the annual fireworks display. Its annual budget of $2.5 million serves nearly 800,000 visitors. Truly, the river is as never before a highway, not for transportation, but for pleasure and entertainment.

Altogether, more than $600 million of national, state, and private funds have made the Connecticut River, according to Spence Conley of the U.S. Fish and Wildlife Service, "the miracle recovery story in the U.S." No other river, he added, had suffered more pollution and abuse from 1750 to the early 1900s. And the Nature Conservancy has designated the 30 miles in the estuary as "one of the last great places on earth."

HOUSES OF CARDS

Buildings Collapse
1978 and 1987

The seer Jeane Dixon predicted it would happen. It could have been the worst human catastrophe in Connecticut, had it occurred six hours earlier. Fortunately, not one person was injured.

At 4:19 A.M. on Wednesday, January 7, 1978, the huge roof over the three-year-old Civic Center on Asylum Street in Hartford collapsed into the arena below with a prolonged rumble that ended in a boom. Once a major engineering feat—the largest single span ever lifted into place—the "space frame" became a twisted mass of steel as it sank to the Coliseum floor 85 feet below.

Later that morning, Joel Lang, ace reporter for the *Hartford Courant*, interviewed firsthand observers, like George Taylor. The sixty-nine-year-old retired manager of the shabby Hartford Hotel that used to stand at the corner of Ann and Church Streets, had agreed to fill in as night clerk. He was watching a snowplow through a window when he felt a tremor and heard a sound something like a big firecracker under a tin can. He rubbed his eyes in disbelief. He said later, "You read about these things, you watch them on television, but when you see one, well, if a drunk had seen it, he would give up liquor!"

Sitting in the cashier's booth at the city parking garage across Church Street, eighteen-year-old Anthony Scheff heard a roar like thunder and turned around to see debris falling. "It took the breath out of me. I was wondering which way to run, because I thought it was the garage." Another employee at the garage, David Smith, said "the first thing I thought was earthquake. I looked at my watch as I started to dive under the counter. It was 4:19."

The roof collapsed in seconds. The debris fell harmlessly into Church and Ann Streets. Not even a window in a neighboring building was broken. Amazingly, too, the retail section of the Civic Center complex, separated by a common wall, had not been damaged. By 8 A.M., as people noted on their way to work, a payloader had plowed most of the debris into a heap. Scores rode the elevator to the twenty-second floor of the Sheraton Hotel to stare in awe at the destruction below.

Nearly 5,000 spectators who six hours earlier had been watching a college basketball game at the Coliseum, the Civic Center's sports arena, must have suffered a visceral shock when they read in the paper how close they came to being buried under 1,400 tons of steel beams. After touring the site, Gov. Ella Grasso told the press, "I can't begin to tell you the absolute horror of it. When you begin to think if people were in there . . ."

Grim city officials gathered in the early morning darkness to view the rubble that had been the foundation of the second stage of a downtown revival. Twisted steel filled the bowl, and broken fixtures littered corridors. They were already talking about rebuilding, and that afternoon the city council committed itself to "an even greater civic center." City Manager James

B. Daken pledged that "it's going to be bigger and better and have a different roof." The business community promised an all-out effort to aid the reconstruction, as did the governor. Arthur J. Lumsden, president of the Greater Hartford Chamber of Commerce, said the collapse should be viewed "not as a catastrophe but as an opportunity to make the rebuilt facility bigger and better."

The Civic Center, completed in 1975 at a cost of $30.5 million, was the second major redevelopment project in downtown Hartford. The first was Constitution Plaza, opened in 1964. Both were spearheaded by Lumsden, whom many looked upon as "King Arthur" because of his success in uniting and presiding over the leading CEOs, who created an agenda of economic and social action. Lumsden first persuaded the Travelers Insurance Company to invest $60 million in replacing a once-vibrant ethnic neighborhood with a complex of modern office buildings. Then, so insiders said, in 1965 he called up the chairman of the Aetna Life Insurance Company, Olcott D. Smith, and told him it was the Aetna's turn to do something big for Hartford. The result was the Civic Center, a complex that besides the Coliseum comprised 70,000 feet of exhibition space, seven restaurants, sixty-three retail shops, and the Sheraton-Hartford Hotel. Financially, the shopping mall was never profitable.

The Coliseum roof, supported only by massive columns at each corner, had been designed to provide an unobstructed view from every seat. When one corner fell in, the resulting compression of air inside the arena apparently ripped loose the rest. Engineers confirmed there was no structural damage to the wall dividing the Coliseum from the adjoining mall, with its retail shops and exhibition halls underneath.

Yet there was a serious economic impact to be faced: the loss of the hockey rink used by the New England Whalers, the major tenant; 300 part-time employees in the Coliseum laid off; and the loss of business for restaurants downtown. At the time the Whalers were in first place, tops in the league in attendance. Assistant coach Don Blackburn was philosophical: "I guess the only thing out of it is that it will give them a chance to put extra seats in the Coliseum when it is rebuilt."

The collapse revived rumors and reports that had begun in 1972, at the beginning of construction, about faulty design. Some said the roof started sagging as soon as it was hoisted in place, and that a "dimple" had formed in the center that supported a heavy scoreboard. Others suspected the drains had become clogged, causing pipes to burst, but City Hall claimed they had been checked three weeks earlier. The most likely cause, an overload of wet snow, was also refuted. Nicholas R. Carbone, the deputy mayor, said the city had been assured by the architects and engineers involved and by its own computer study that the roof would stand up to any weight. "We've had heavier weight on the roof than this," he argued. Despite heavy snow during January of 1978, the most it could have weighed was 24.5 pounds per square foot, less than the 30 pounds engineered by the designers Philip Wesler and Werner Blum.

Beginning in February and continuing into May, Room 211 on the second floor of Hartford's City Hall was occupied by a three-person council committee appointed to investigate the disaster. The only physical evidence of what happened was a row of five red seats salvaged from the wreckage. At the head of the conference table was chairwoman Barbara B. Kennelly, daughter of the late Democratic Party boss John M. Bailey, and subsequently the popular congresswoman from the First

Timing is everything—six hours before the Civic Center collapsed, 5,000 people were there for a basketball game. CONNECTICUT HISTORICAL SOCIETY MUSEUM

District. Freshman councilman Sidney L. Gardner, a consultant on urban problems, sat next to her. He found the investigation a perfect case study of modern government. "I knew this was going to be an engineering undertaking of enormous complexity, and it had to be handled like in medicine when you've got elective surgery. You never take a single doctor's opinion." The third committee member was Democrat Raymond Montero, a roofer and carpenter. The chief counsel was John S. Murtha. The committee heard thirty-nine witnesses and saw 215 exhibits. Testimony and questions filled 2,200 pages of transcripts.

The committee retained Charles H. Thornton, president of Lev Zetlin Associates, as an independent investigator. His 400-page report was released on June 16. The highlights:

- The initiating cause of the collapse was a deficient design related to inadequate bracing.
- A major contributing cause was underestimation by 1.5 million pounds of the total loads—i.e., the total weight bearing on the structure—bringing the total weight to 20 percent higher than the engineers' design allowed for.
- The extra loads resulted from added roofing materials and steel for catwalks and lights.
- The live weight of snow accounted for only twelve pounds per square foot, compared with the total dead load of sixty-six pounds, close to capacity.
- Design and inspection procedures were inadequate.
- A design and code review by either the city or an outside consultant would have detected the design deficiencies.

The rebuilt Coliseum was, as promised, bigger and better. It seats 14,500. Instead of the original space frame, the new roof is supported by a series of trusses that look like huge ladders with diagonal rungs, similar to the supports on bridges. Overall, the Civic Center has undergone a major transformation. In place of the mall there's a thirty-story skyscraper with apartments and stores that opened in 2006.

In the spring of 1987, the citizens of Bridgeport were watching the erection of the largest residential apartment complex the city had seen in two decades on Washington Avenue. The complex, a central part of the city's hoped-for renaissance, had the lofty name of L'Ambiance Plaza. It was designed to have thirteen stories and a five-story adjoining parking garage. About 1:30 P.M. on Thursday, April 23, the structure collapsed as some of the seventy-one workers were lifting huge concrete slabs. Under this construction process prepoured concrete slabs were placed in position above one another by means of hydraulic jacks. Fifteen workers were killed immediately and thirteen more never accounted for.

"It's a sight out of Beirut, Lebanon," moaned Mayor Thomas W. Bucci. "That's the only way I can describe it, a bombing in Beirut." The manager of a nearby store, Vincent DiScala, said, "the ground shook and then it was followed by a sound like an explosion. We looked out and the building just went down out of sight. We had been watching that building go up, and in a matter of seconds it disappeared." A city building inspector, Frank Mercaldi, said he had visited the site on Monday and saw no problems. The lift-slab process in his opinion was totally acceptable; it had been used to erect Bridgeport's new Hilton Hotel and the Innwood Apartments on Park Avenue.

Accounts of the collapse varied. Some compared it with a bomb explosion, others to an earthquake. Residents of nearby apartments said the force shook their buildings, and when they raced outdoors, they were greeted by a thick, choking cloud of dust. From his first floor apartment across the street, Jesus Rivera had kept his eyes on the building rising floor by floor, month by month. "I didn't give it a second thought when I looked at it about 10 minutes before. I saw a few guys on the third floor and six on the top. And then I was fixing lunch and it sounded like an explosion."

A plumber, Joe Murzyn, barely escaped with his life. The day before, he had not reported for work because he was "a little leery" about the safety of the slabs.

> We called it the International House of Pancakes because we knew if one of those floors came down, it's gonna be disastrous, and it happened. We heard the top floor hit the floor below it and, boom, I knew it was coming down. I just dove for my life into the ditch, about 18 feet below.

Rodney House, an ironworker, had been watching the pouring of cement on the fourth floor and then descended to the basement; within five minutes he heard a big crack, then another. He started running. Outside, the force of the falling slabs lifted him off the ground and threw him into a dirt bank 5 feet away. "It's unbelievable, the power of it. It blew me like you blow a feather in the wind." He was unhurt.

Terence Williams, a plumber on the second floor who was erecting hangers, felt the floor shaking violently, and seconds later he was falling 30 feet into the basement. A thick chalky fog of concrete dust blinded him. "I didn't know what happened," he said. Charles Lorello, a carpenter, missed death by a second. He had just finished showing his boss, Dick McGill, where he planned to install metal walls the next day, and both men were walking out to put drill-gun parts into McGill's van, Lorello in front, McGill behind. The next instant McGill vanished, presumably buried.

As the gray day wore on, the crowd on the sidewalks grew larger. Tradesmen from other building sites joined police and paramedics to begin rescue work, bringing cutting and lifting equipment. The state police brought dogs trained to sniff out buried bodies; others tried sensitive underground listening devices and miniature infrared video cameras, without success. Driven by reports of noises emanating from the rubble, all struggled furiously in the rain through Thursday and around the clock on Friday to pull apart the mountain of debris. Some searchers described tapping sounds; others said they heard moans. Still others feared the sounds were nothing more than settling concrete. No survivors were found.

Gov. William A. O'Neill, who had been attending a conference in Stamford, rushed to the scene Thursday. He feared there was little hope any of the missing would be found alive. Investigators from the federal Occupational Heath and Safety Administration soon arrived to determine the cause. Late Thursday, the "Plaza" resembled some sort of grotesque, futuristic sculpture. Bright yellow light from sodium vapor lamps bathed massive chunks of broken concrete and twisted girders, as the hard hats cut through girders and backhoes loaded loose concrete into trucks. An Episcopal priest, the Reverend Timothy B. Safford, tried to comfort the relatives who stood around helpless. As he recalled:

> It's a communication mess. It just wrenches your guts. People were saying to me "why wasn't God there to protect them?" I couldn't chide them for asking the question. You just tell them God will be with them.

Building procedures and soil problems were cited by investigators and experts as the likely causes of the collapse. The Connecticut Housing Finance Authority, which had provided $15 million in low-interest loans to finance the $17.5 million project, said a structural engineer was concerned that holes in the concrete slabs had been planned too close to the steel columns that supported the building. One contractor reported that "there are certain shear walls and slab openings that do not conform with the dimensions indicated on the contract documents."

Design plans called for "undisturbed rock" to support the load of seven tons per square foot. An engineer hired by the *Courant* said the records show the building was being erected on a site composed of compacted earth and broken rock, the kind of fill that cannot support more than four tons per square foot. This might have caused the footings to settle and increase stress. No record had been filed at Bridgeport City Hall to show that proper testing had been done. Other engineers and architects familiar with the lift-slab process pointed to three different possibilities: instability in the steel columns, weakness on the concrete slabs, and failure to jack the load evenly.

The L'Ambiance Plaza collapse was reminiscent of two other construction disasters. In 1941, during the building of the new Charter Oak Bridge over the Connecticut River in Hartford, a span gave way and killed fifteen workers. It was soon repaired, and the bridge opened the next year. On June 28, 1983, the Mianus Bridge in Greenwich broke apart and took three lives.

DRIVE SAFELY

Highway Tragedies
1983 and 2005

Fatalities are everyday occurrences on our crowded highways, but collisions resulting in multiple deaths are mercifully rare. Three of the notable ones in Connecticut were the crash at the Stratford tollbooth and the collapse of the Mianus Bridge, both in 1983, and the horrendous accident at the foot of Avon Mountain in 2005.

On Wednesday, January 11, 1983, around 3 P.M., a tractor-trailer slammed into a car waiting in a tollbooth line in the eastbound lane of Interstate 95, and was then struck from behind by another car. The vehicles burst into flames, destroying the cars. The fire was so intense the registration plates were illegible. Six passengers were incinerated. The bodies were taken to the state medical examiner's office in Farmington, where dental records were used to identify them.

Just as he was going off duty, John Leslie, a toll collector, pulled a young boy out of the front seat of one car that had overturned; the boy later died in the hospital. Leslie said, "I had my back turned to the lanes when I heard a smash." Turning around, he saw a cloud of smoke and flames and the upside-down car compacted with the tractor-trailer. The driver of the tractor-trailer, Charles L. Kurtz, thirty-five, was injured and had to undergo surgery. Police determined that his truck had entered one of the exact change lanes reserved for cars only and should not have been there.

Traffic on the busy interstate was tied up for hours, as the bodies were removed and the rubble across five lanes cleaned up. Secondary roads were quickly clogged, causing mammoth bottlenecks. The accident renewed pleas from lawmakers who for a long time had urged the removal of tollbooths because of pollution and safety problems. A bill to do this had passed the Connecticut State House the previous year but narrowly failed in the senate. State Rep. J. Vincent Chase of Stratford, who spearheaded their unsuccessful fight in the legislature, wondered "how many more of these deaths do we have to face?" Long-time state senator George L. Gunther agreed. "These things [toll stations] ought to be out of there." However, Gov. William O'Neill remained in opposition. Finally, on December 31, 1985, the tollbooths were removed from the Connecticut Turnpike and on June 24, 1988, from the Merritt and Wilbur Cross Parkways.

Only the State Department of Transportation knew that some of the 3,425 bridges in Connecticut were in need of repair. In 1979 department commissioner Arthur B. Powers warned that "the potential for a major catastrophe from a bridge failure increases daily." Previously, there had been only one other bridge disaster: during construction in 1941 the center span of the Charter Oak Bridge in Hartford collapsed, killing fifteen men; a new bridge opened the next year.

Then on a sultry night on June 28, 1983, his warning became a reality in Greenwich when a 100-foot span of the Connecticut Turnpike fell into the Mianus River. Four vehicles plunged into the muddy water 70 feet below. Three lives were lost and three other persons were seriously injured, one of whom would be crippled for life. Had the collapse occurred during daylight, when 90,000 vehicles normally crossed, going south or north, the casualty count would certainly have been much higher and possibly the state's worst highway accident.

On the river cabin cruisers were rocking gently at their berths in the Cos Cob yacht harbor. It was 1:30 A.M. Most of those aboard were asleep. The peace of the summer night was shattered by a crash followed by screams. "It was like an earthquake," said Bill Ebrech of Yonkers, New York. "The whole boat rumbled." Shaken awake, he saw a nightmarish sight, 200 yards from his boat. In a truck's cab, waist deep in the water, sat a man and a women who were covered with blood. Bill Ebrech reached out to help them. They were David and Helen Pace, a recently married truck-driving couple from Warner-Robins, Georgia, who were hauling a load of empty bottles. Walking on their heels and pressing their backs against the trailer, the Paces inched their way to Ebrech's boat. Once in, Mrs. Pace sat and her husband lay down. They were all in shock. She muttered "Thanks!"

Within ten minutes of the collapse, police and firefighters arrived on the eastern shore, only 30 feet away. The three injured were dragged from the shallow water, near where the broken span had landed intact. Two 45-foot sections of roadway, attached to columns on either side, were left hanging.

Twenty-year-old Emilio Alvarez-Recio was sitting with friends on his parents' boat in the Harbor Marine Center, next to the bridge, when he heard "an enormous metal-crunching sound." He said, "The splash was incredible. The whole thing was like an explosion. That's when we saw a car going over." Brakes screeched, tail lights went over the bridge and disappeared, and then other cars and trucks behind stopped, and their drivers got out and looked down.

Mary Oldman, who lived 200 feet away, said it sounded like thunder. Her husband Arthur, an insurance broker, added, "We have seen in the past pieces of metal beams hang and later fall from the bridge, and one of our neighborhood boys was narrowly missed by a hunk of falling concrete." His neighbor, Gordon Gilman, whose house was for sale, said all the neighbors had been especially concerned in recent weeks, because the bridge seemed noisier and was vibrating more often than in the past.

Two of the victims were from Stamford: Luis Kapata, age thirty-one, the driver of a BMW that sailed off the bridge and landed several hundred feet under the farther side, and his passenger, Reginald K. Fischer, age twenty-one. The other fatality was a truck driver, Harold W. Bracy Jr., forty-five, from Santa Ana, California. He was carrying a load of meat from Dumas, Texas, to a Stop & Shop store in Hartford. In addition to the Paces, Eileen Weldon, of Darien, a twenty-one-year-old student at George Washington University, was badly injured when her car landed upside-down on top of the collapsed span. Three years later, she still suffered from the effects of fractures of her spine, collarbone, shoulder blade, and left arm, and was paralyzed on the left side of her body.

A weary young couple in a Nissan Sentra looking for a place to spend the night after attending a baseball game in New York had a narrow escape. William Anderson and Shannon Kelly got lost trying to get out of the city. Shannon was trying to read two maps in her lap as they approached Cos Cob. Suddenly, in the middle of the bridge the lights went out. Anderson managed to brake 10 feet from the edge, just behind a tractor-trailer in the center lane. "My first thought was that we were going to be in a bad wreck, a three- or four-car accident. Then I saw the cab facing us and knew it was jackknifing. It disappeared and I heard a scraping sound of metal on metal." Fearing that other cars would drive over the edge, but afraid of being hit himself, Anderson, who'd gotten out of his car, stood at the median, waving his arms and yelling. A car whizzed past (Kapata and Fischer). "They didn't stop. I don't know why." It was a futile warning that haunted him for a long time. Next came a truck that Anderson was able to flag down; the driver turned on his flashers and blocked other traffic. He also called for help on his CB radio.

Later in the morning, traffic was rerouted on I–95 in both directions. The accident scene had a surreal look with the three northbound lanes sheared off abruptly, a blue work shirt dangling over the precipice, heavy black skid marks on the pavement, and dents in the guardrail. The state police underwater team recovered broken structural components from the river's bottom. Bulldozers from the Department of Consumer Protection were pushing debris onto garbage trucks. On Wednesday a New Jersey firm started to erect a temporary bridge over the river. Officials hoped the new structure would be ready to carry passenger cars in two weeks.

The collapse of the Mianus Bridge aroused the public's fears. How many other bridges in the state were overloaded or poorly maintained? The Department of Transportation quickly pointed out that Mianus, built in 1958, had been inspected the

previous September over a three-day period and found struc-
turally sound. Yet its rating on a scale of zero to nine was
three—the lowest rating for a bridge allowed to remain open.
Attention focused on a pin 7 inches in diameter that helped
hold the pavement in place. At a news conference the DOT
commissioner, J. William Burns, admitted that "this pin is a
significant part of our concerns. If it was missing or sheared
off, it could have caused this collapse." Pins were integral to
the expanding joints placed at four points; they were inserted
in opposite ends of 4-foot "hangers" that held the beams
together. Thomas Kuesel, the head of a leading New York
bridge engineering firm, called bridges of the hanging-pin
design "problem children." "Over the years," he said, "they
have tended to give maintenance difficulties."

In response to an invitation from the National Transportation Safety Board for information, DOT immediately undertook
an in-house investigation. Completed in December, it concluded that

> the cause of the collapse was due to stresses which were not
> considered in the design of the bridge. These stresses acting
> continually over an extended period of time, resulted in lat-
> eral movements of the pin and hanger assemblies which
> were not designed to withstand such forces.

The DOT also retained Hardesty & Hanover, a nationally
recognized bridge consulting firm from New York City, to provide emergency services for both the restoration of the Mianus
Bridge and for the safety inspection of forty-eight suspended-
type spans elsewhere in the state. DOT inspectors were diverted
from their regular assignments to conduct detailed inspections

on another twenty-five similar spans. None of the seventy-three spans were found deficient. At the same time bridge inspection policies and procedures were reviewed, and the review was backed up by outside consultants. Their report in July 1984 cited the lack of a single bridge authority and recommended combining all the functions under an engineer of bridges.

In October Gov. William A. O'Neill called a special session of the legislature to take action, two years overdue, on the DOT's chronic complaints about lack of funds for bridge inspection and repair, roadway resurfacing, and truck weight enforcement. Responding to the pleas of Commissioner Burns, it approved, as part of a ten-year, $5.5 billion-dollar program, $41 million to enable Burns to commence the repair or replacement of 470 bridges rated to be in fair or poor condition.

The state filed a $25 million suit against the New York bridge designers, contending that the design was unusual and unsafe. A consultant's report, for which the state paid $800,000 in 1985, echoing the DOT's conclusions, laid the blame for the accident solely on design flaws. Discounting maintenance problems as a contributing cause, the report claimed that the sharp angle of the bridge's supporting piers created sideways pressures that disengaged a critical pin and hanger assembly. At the trial the defense argued that state inspectors had neglected to inspect the rusted assembly closely. "They had control of the bridge for 25 years. . . . When built, it was a proper, appropriate, safe and usable design." A six-man jury agreed. In 1986 the state paid $7.8 million in out of court settlements and laid out $17.4 million to repair the Mianus Bridge.

U.S. Highway 44 over the 600-foot-high Avon Mountain from West Hartford to Avon is the main commuting route from

Hartford to the western suburbs. It is notorious for its dangers, a curving climb or descent in both directions, with many blind turns into side streets. Oblivious of the dangers, vehicles often travel much too fast. In winter time the hazards are doubled. For years the public had clamored for action to make the highway safer. No major improvement has been made.

On a clear, dry morning, July 29, 2005, a loaded dump truck traveling west on US 44 spun out of control as it rounded the last curve, braking for the traffic light at the intersection with Route 10. "It was just flying, careening down the hill," said Richard D. Frieder, a librarian at the Hartford Public Library, waiting in the front row of four lanes for the light to turn green. "The timing was so split second. It was starting to tip over . . . and pretty much coming at me. I actually called out, to no one, oh shit! Then there was impact." Frieder's car was sideswiped by another on his left that the runaway truck had hit first, then it tipped over on two wheels. Frieder climbed out the passenger side and looking back saw what he aptly called "carnage." Screaming for help amid the flames consuming his truck, the driver, Abdulraheem Naafi, age forty-one, burned to death.

Mary Murray, in a Kelly Transit commuter bus on her way to work at Cigna, sitting near the front, saw the dump truck veering across the intersection. "I'm thinking, that's going to be a bad accident, but it's not going to affect us because we're too far back." She was wrong: Something flew up and shattered the front window. The bus driver lay on the floor unconscious. Murray escaped through a side window onto a wrecked car; a man told her to jump into his arms. She called the scene "horrific, a scene from Baghdad, a bombing, exactly what you see on TV every day."

Mark DiPinto of Burlington was riding to work with a neighbor, Jennifer Spielman. Seeing the truck, she pulled her Audi convertible to the right. The collision's chain reaction covered them with dirt. "We had half an inch of topsoil on our backs," he said. He began helping people out of the Kelly bus, which was still in gear, its wheels spinning, and lurching repeatedly into the cars ahead. He managed to drag the injured driver out. "The overall scene," he added," looked like a plane wreck; 100 yards of mess."

As gasoline tanks exploded and caught fire, dazed motorists exited their cars; others were in such shock they could not move. Those uninjured ran to help the injured. Among them was West Hartford police officer Todd Myers. He was stunned by the devastation. Grabbing his portable radio, he told his dispatcher to notify the Avon police. Soon, two Life Star rescue helicopters appeared and took three seriously injured persons to Hartford Hospital. Rescue workers from half a dozen towns descended on the scene, closed off the intersection, and redirected traffic.

There were many heroic rescuers that Friday, but one in particular was amazing. A fifty-year-old professor of surgery, Dr. Scott Kurtsman, en route from Simsbury to lecture medical students at the UConn Health Center in Farmington, was idling his car in the far right lane, waiting to turn onto Route 10. He swung hard onto the Nassau furniture store lawn. "The truck driver apparently tried to avoid the cars headed westbound by swerving around them," he said. "My guess is he didn't have brakes." He raced to help the driver, but there was no getting him out. "The truck was so engulfed in flames I couldn't get within 15 feet." Then he helped Todd Myers pull a woman out of her car by cutting her seat belt. "At that point there was a lot of chaos, a lot of stuff happening," the doctor said. They carried the woman to the lawn and ran to the next car closest to the burning truck. The next thing he remembered, besides the intense heat, he was working on two of the rescued, while paramedics and bystanders brought more people to him. "We were trying to figure out who was alive and get them stabilized and to hospitals as fast as we could." The Reverend Jon Widing, chaplain of the Avon Police Department, watched in awe as Kurtsman moved from one victim to another. Widing said, "He was quite spectacular, calm and cool." When he had done all he could, the doctor retrieved his car and continued to the Medical Center, where he changed his bloody clothes for surgical scrubs and started his lecture, only an hour late.

In a few seconds that morning, four died and nineteen were injured. Though the charred vehicles were cleared off Friday night, Saturday revealed obvious reminders of what had happened: chunks of gray-black asphalt, grapefruit-size rocks and clumps of dirt next to Nassau's furniture store, faint odors of burned tires and oil. Someone had placed a bouquet of orange flowers at the base of a utility pole, and a nurse, Kathleen O'Brien of Farmington, laid another bouquet on the shards of glass still strewn in the grass.

The aftermath proved to be as intriguing a story as the collision itself. The first question investigators sought to answer was why the Mack truck spun out of control: Was it brake failure or driver incompetence? The truth emerged bit by bit in the following days. The truck, owned by American Crushing & Recycling of Bloomfield, had been taken out of service by state inspectors the year before because of a power-steering fluid leak and brakes that were out of adjustment. Three months later, another spot check found the leak had not been repaired.

Delving into state records, the *Hartford Courant* discovered that roadside truck inspections had dropped 30 percent from 2000 to 2004, prompting Gov. Jodi Rell to order Ralph J. Carpenter, the DMV commissioner, to increase the number of safety inspectors immediately.

Next, eyes focused on the driver's record. Three days before the tragedy, Naafi, aka Terrance Stokes, had been fired from another trucking company because of unreliable work habits and improper operation of its vehicles. He also was facing charges of drug possession. His criminal record dated to the mid-1980s. He began working at American Crushing & Recycling on Wednesday. His assignment Friday had been to haul fill to a construction site on Deercliff Road at the top of Avon Mountain. For an unknown reason he missed the left turn from Route 44 onto Deercliff and instead careened down the steep grade to his doom.

It was to be expected that legislators and officials would clamor for immediate safety improvements, such as more speed warning signs, widening the highway to add breakdown lanes, and a ramp for runaway trucks. A state senator, Jonathan Harris of West Hartford, asked why signs hadn't been ordered for the downhill stretch on the east side. He recalled that only a few weeks previously a poultry truck barely missed ramming cars at the intersection with Mountain Road. State transportation crews began trimming branches and brush along the sides. Letters to the media urged that trucks be banned on the mountain altogether and, to achieve the ultimate solution, that a tunnel be dug under the mountain. Another fantasy was DOT's proposal that a $20 million bridge be built over Route 10/Nod Road.

Because the company was not insured, in October Superior Court Judge John J. Langenbach appointed a receiver to manage

American Crushing and sell its assets. Calling the ruling "one of the most blatant denials of due process in the history of Connecticut," David Wilcox's lawyer—Wilcox was the owner of American Crushing—Hubert J. Santos, claimed "there's never been a finding as to the cause of this accident. In fact what happened here was driver error. This driver couldn't figure out how to downshift that vehicle and blew the engine." He added that Naafi had done the same thing to a Lyons Company truck a week earlier.

In November fraud reared its ugly head. David Wilcox was taken into custody on charges he tried to reinstate liability insurance on his truck hours *after* it crashed. His wife, the office manager, was also implicated. A conviction could result in prison sentences of up to forty-five years. Apparently, in January 2005 Mrs. Wilcox had requested their insurance agent cancel the coverage on all of their twelve trucks. An hour after the accident, she called the insurance agency to get the policy reinstated effective at 12:01 A.M. July 29. Around 10:30 her husband notified Webster Insurance that one of his trucks had been involved in a fatal crash. In the afternoon he presented a liability insurance card to an Avon police officer. Wilcox's arrest came the same day the governor signed into law a measure that made it a felony for commercial vehicle owners to operate without liability insurance.

The *Courant* editorialized that the Avon crash was "a disaster waiting to happen." And it did.

Bibliography

TRAITOROUS FIRE
The Burning of New London (1781)

Caulkins, Frances M. *History of New London, Connecticut.* New London: H. D. Utley, 1895.

Connecticut Courant. September 11, 1781.

Powell, Walter L. *Murder or Mayhem? Benedict Arnold's New London, Connecticut Raid, 1781.* Gettysburg, Penn.: Thomas Publications, 2000.

SHAKES AND MOANS
The Moodus Earthquake (1791)

Bell, Michael. *The Face of Connecticut.* Hartford: Department of Environmental Protection, 1985.

Clemons, W. H. "The Legends of Machimoodus," *Connecticut* magazine, vol. 7, pp. 454–58, 1903.

Parket, Francis H. "Moodus Noises," Connecticut Historical Society manuscript.

THE BRITISH ARE COMING!
The Raid on Essex (1814)

"Captain Richard Coote's Report," *Connecticut Gazette,* April 13, 1814.

Delaney, Edmund Thomas. *The Connecticut River: New England's Historic Waterway.* Chester, Conn.:, The Globe Pequot Press, 1983.

Grant, Ellsworth S. *Thar She Goes!* Essex and Lyme: Connecticut River Museum and Greenwich Publications, 2000.

SMOKE ON THE WATER
Deadly Steamboats (1833 and 1840)

Coroner's Proceedings, New York. "Explosion of the Lexington,"
    pamphlet, Hartford: Connecticut Historical Society, November
    1940.
Lazell, Warren. "Explosion of the *New England,*" in *Steamboat*
    Disasters & Accidents. Essex: Connecticut River Museum,
    Essex, Conn., pp. 155–63.

CURSED LITTLE DITCH
The Ill-Fated Farmington Canal (1835)

Bickford, Christopher. *Farmington in Connecticut.* Canaan, N.H.:
    Phoenix Publications, 1982.
Clark, George L. *A History of Connecticut.* New York: Putnam's Sons,
    1914.
Osterweis, Rollin G. *Three Centuries of New Haven.* New Haven,
    Conn.: Yale University Press, 1953.

THE RESCUE OF KIDNAPPED AFRICANS
The *Amistad* Affair (1839)

Bickford, Christopher. *Farmington in Connecticut.* Canaan, N.H.:
    Phoenix Publications, 1982.
McCain, Diana R. *Free Men: The* Amistad *Revolt and the American*
    Anti-Slavery Movement. New Haven, Conn.: New Haven Histori-
    cal Society, 1990.
Owens, William A. *Black Mutiny: The Revolt of the Schooner Amistad.*
    Baltimore: Black Classics Press, 1997.

BRIDGE OUT!
The Norwalk Train Wreck (1853)

Mittelmann, Michael M. "Dr. Gurdon W. Russell's Account of the
1853 Railroad Accident," *Connecticut Medicine,* vol. 64, no. 5,
pp. 291–297, May 2000.
Turner, Gregg M. and Melancthon W. Jacobus. *Connecticut
Railroads.* Hartford: Connecticut Historical Society, 1986.

THAT DEMON, STEAM!
The Fales & Gray Explosion (1854)

Grant, Ellsworth S. *The Colt Legacy: The Story of the Colt Armory in
Hartford, 1855–1980,* 2nd ed. Woonsocket, R.I.: Mowbray,
1995.

GUNS BLAZING
The Colt Armory Fire (1864)

Grant, Ellsworth S. *The Colt Legacy: The Story of the Colt Armory in
Hartford, 1855–1980,* 2nd ed. Woonsocket, R.I.: Mowbray,
1995.
Hartford Courant. February 13, 1864, p. 8 ff.

AN ICY PLUNGE
The Tariffville Bridge Wreck (1878)

Turner, Gregg M. and Melancthon W. Jacobus. *Connecticut
Railroads.* Hartford: Connecticut Historical Society, 1986.

LET IT SNOW, LET IT SNOW, LET IT SNOW
The Great Blizzard (1888)

Grant, Ellsworth S. *The Colt Legacy: The Story of the Colt Armory in
Hartford, 1855–1980,* 2nd ed. Woonsocket, R.I.: Mowbray,
1995.
Hartford Courant. March 12, 1888 & ff.

THINGS THAT GO BANG! IN THE NIGHT
The Park Central Explosion (1889)

Hartford Courant. February 18, 1889.

WORSE THAN WORLD WAR I
The Influenza Epidemic (1918–1919)

Arcari, Ralph D., and Hudson Birden. "The 1918 Influenza
Epidemic in Connecticut," *Connecticut Medical Quarterly,* 1999,
pp. 28–42.
Connecticut State Department of Health. "The Epidemic of
Influenza in Connecticut." *State Department of Health Bulletin,*
vol. 33, no. 4, April 1919.
"Influenza Epidemic of 1918–1919." Annual report of the State
Department of Health.

EVEN COLT GOT SOAKED
The Great Flood (1936)

Grant, Ellsworth S. *A Connecticut Journey.* West Hartford: Wood
Pond Press, 2004.

THE BIGGEST BLOW OF THEM ALL
The Great Hurricane (1938)

Grant, Ellsworth S. "My Sister-in-Law," in *A Connecticut Journey.*
West Hartford: Wood Pond Press, 2004, pp. 144–153.
Hepburn, Katharine. *Me: Stories of My Life.* New York: Random
House, 1996.
Manchester, William. *The Glory and the Dream: A Narrative History
of America, 1932–1972.* Boston: Little, Brown and Company,
1974.
Scotti, R. A. *Sudden Sea.* Boston: Little, Brown and Company, 2003.

A THREE-RING HORROR
The Hartford Circus Fire (1944)

Hartford Courant. July 7, 1944 & ff.
Hartford Times. July 7, 1944 & ff.
O'Nan, Stewart. *The Circus Fire.* New York: Doubleday, 2000.

THE SNEAKY SUPER STORM
Hurricanes Connie and Diane (1955)

Hartford Courant, August 21, 1955 & ff.
———. "John Hersey's Story," August 28, 1955.

A NEW YEAR'S EVE NIGHTMARE
The Cathedral Fire (1956)

Grant, Ellsworth S. *A Connecticut Journey.* West Hartford:
Wood Pond Press, 2004.
Hartford Courant. January 1, 1957.

MEDICAL CENTER MALADY
The Hartford Hospital Fire (1961)

Hartford Courant. December 1961, pp. 9–12.

THE RESCUE OF A RIVER
Connecticut River Pollution (1965)

Grant, Ellsworth S. *A Connecticut Journey.* West Hartford:
    Wood Pond Press, 2004.

HOUSES OF CARDS
Buildings Collapse (1978 and 1987)

Hartford Courant. "Civic Center Collapse," January 18, 1978.
————. "L'Ambiance Plaza Collapse," April 23, 1987.

DRIVE SAFELY
Highway Tragedies (1983 and 2005)

Connecticut State Department of Transportation. *Findings, Conclu-
    sions, and Recommendations of Mianus Bridge Collapse,* Hartford:
    Connecticut DOT, December 1983.
Hartford Courant. "Stratford Toll Booth Crash," January 11, 1983.
————. "Mianus Bridge Collapse," June 29, 1983.
————. "Avon Mountain Tragedy," July 30, 2005.

A portion of Chapter 6 was originally published in *The* Amistad *Revolt and the American Anti-Slavery Movement* by Diana McCain. Reprinted by permission of the Connecticut Historical Society.

Portions of Chapters 7 and 10 were originally published in *Connecticut Railroads* by Gregg M. Turner and Melancthon W. Jacobus. Reprinted by permission of the Connecticut Historical Society.

Portions of Chapters 8 and 9 were originally published in *The Colt Armory* by Ellsworth S. Grant. Reprinted by permission of the author.

Portions of Chapters 14 and 15 were originally published in *A Connecticut Journey* by Ellsworth S. Grant. Reprinted by permission of the author.

About the Author

Lifelong Connecticut resident Ellsworth S. Grant has been a manufacturer, mayor of West Hartford (1969–1973), personnel director, educational film producer, president of the Connecticut Historical Society, and brother-in-law to the legendary Katharine Hepburn. Born in Wethersfield, he attended Kingswood-Oxford School in West Hartford and graduated from Harvard in 1939. The son of the president of Allen Manufacturer Company (which made various kinds of fasteners, including the "Allen wrench"), Ellsworth went into a career in manufacturing. In his second career as a writer, much of his work has covered Connecticut's history of manufacturing, such as in *The Colt Armory*. Two of his best-known books are *Yankee Dreamers and Doers*, published by Pequot Press in 1974, and *The Miracle of Connecticut*, the second edition of which was published by the Connecticut Historical Society and Fenwick Productions. In collaboration with his first wife, Marion Hepburn, he wrote *The City of Hartford* (1986), a pictorial history. Before *Connecticut Disasters*, his most recent book was his 2004 autobiography *A Connecticut Journey* (Wood Pond Press). He is a lifelong sailing enthusiast on the Long Island Sound and a contributor to various magazines, including *American Heritage, Northeast, Hartford*, and *Cruising World*.